THE SECRET &
LILY HART

TWO TALES BY
CHARLOTTE BRONTË

TRANSCRIBED FROM THE ORIGINAL
MANUSCRIPT AND EDITED BY
WILLIAM HOLTZ

UNIVERSITY OF MISSOURI PRESS
COLUMBIA & LONDON
1979

Illustrations

Grateful acknowledgment is given to The Brontë Society, Haworth, for granting permission to use the illustrations shown on the following pages: pp. 1, 6, 8, 12, 14, 31, 32

Library of Congress Cataloging in Publication Data

Brontë, Charlotte, 1816–1855.
    The secret & Lily Hart.
    Contains facsimile texts and edited texts of both works.
    1. Brontë, Charlotte, 1816–1855—Manuscripts—Facsimiles. I. Holtz, William V. II. Brontë, Charlotte, 1816–1855. Lily Hart. 1979. III. Title.
PZ3.B790Sf 1979 [PR4166] 823'.8 78-19645
ISBN 0-8262-0268-3

FINALLY,

A BOOK FOR

ERICA AND

SIGRID ...

Acknowledgments   I would like to thank the following people for their help at various stages in the preparation of this book. My major obligation is to James W. Symington, whose gift of the Brontë manuscript to the University of Missouri made this undertaking possible. I am indebted to several of my colleagues in the Department of English for their aid and advice: Professors Donald Anderson, Lloyd Berry, J. Donald Crowley, Milton M. Gatch, William Peden, and John R. Roberts. Professor Emerita Mildred Christian of Tulane University and Anthony Garnett were helpful in regard to certain features of the manuscript. Dwight Tuckwood and Margaret Howell of the library staff were trustworthy guardians of the manuscript. Rose McClure, Margaret Butler, and Marjorie Wallace offered me skilled secretarial help when I needed it. Corinne Davis cheerfully typed the difficult final manuscript. Finally, I must mention the many times my wife, Lora, willingly put aside her own work to help me with mine: every page here bears her impress.

I was also materially aided by the Research Council of the University of Missouri–Columbia, who granted me a Summer Research Fellowship for the initial stages of this work and who provided funds for the final preparation of the manuscript.

...ther — Painted by Martin —
...ied by B. B — Brontë — Decr. 1830

Preface   This book is an edition of and a commentary on a tiny manuscript containing "The Secret" and "Lily Hart," two stories that are part of Charlotte Brontë's juvenilia. The manuscript was found among the possessions of Mrs. Evelyn Symington, wife of U.S. Senator Stuart M. Symington, after her death in 1973. It was presented to the University of Missouri in 1975 by U.S. Congressman James W. Symington.

A Note on the Text.   The Brontë juvenilia are characterized by their minute size and almost microscopic handwriting. This particular manuscript consists of no more than four sheets of notepaper folded into a sixteen-page book of $4\frac{1}{2}$ inches long and $3\frac{5}{8}$ inches wide[1] and contains approximately nineteen thousand words. On the title page, Charlotte inscribed the pseudonym "Charles Wellesley," the name she often used in the other juvenilia. "The Secret" begins on page 3 of the manuscript, and "Lily Hart" begins midway through page 11. The last page of text (page 15 of the manuscript) is signed "Charlotte Brontë" and dated "November 7th, —33." She was then seventeen years old.

The reader who turns to the accompanying facsimile will see the problems of editing the Brontë juvenilia. Not only is the script almost microscopic, but the punctuation is rudimentary, often inconsistent, and frequently simply absent. With these difficulties in mind, I have attempted in this edition to serve two readers, not only the accomplished Brontë specialist but also what Samuel Johnson approvingly called "the common reader." For the second I have provided an edited text, supplying punctuation and

---

1. The manuscript, now in the rare book collection of the Elmer Ellis Library, University of Missouri–Columbia, has been cut apart where the notepaper was originally folded, so it appears to be made of eight sheets. Technically, it originally could have been folded and cut from one sheet.

paragraph divisions and normalizing spelling and capitalization to conform to modern British usage. Where the text is obscure, I have indicated my suggested reading with square brackets. Wholly illegible words or passages are similarly indicated. Of course, such editorial normalizing does destroy the unique effect of the tiny manuscript and the sense of feverishly intense composition that its text suggests; thus I have included a facsimile of the manuscript in its entirety. Finally, I have provided introductory material and appendixes that will permit an informed appreciation of these tales in their larger context. The Brontë scholar will have less need for these aids, but he will perhaps find useful the photographic enlargements of the manuscript and my attempt to transcribe the original as accurately as the difficulties of the manuscript allow.

Provenance of the Manuscript. Apparently the first person outside the Brontë family to see this manuscript—or any of the Brontë juvenilia—was Elizabeth Gaskell, who, while gathering material for a biography just after Charlotte's death, visited the Reverend Patrick Brontë, Charlotte's father, and examined some of these early works. She chose to reproduce the first page of "The Secret" to illustrate this phase of Charlotte's work.[2] Since Gaskell's publication of Charlotte's *Life* in 1857, this page has been all that has been known of the manuscript. Presumably it traveled to Ireland with Charlotte's husband, the Reverend Arthur Bell Nicholls, and returned to England among the trove of juvenilia purchased from Nicholls by Clement Shorter in 1895, which passed to T. J. Wise.[3] At this point it probably received its present leather

---

2. Elizabeth Gaskell, *The Life of Charlotte Brontë*, 2 vols. (London, 1857), 1:84.

3. Clement Shorter, *The Brontës: Life and Letters*, 2 vols. (London, 1908; reprinted New York, 1969), 1:19-20; T. J. Wise and J. A. Symington, eds.,

binding, as Wise dispersed many of the individual manuscripts on the marketplace as literary curiosities. This provenance is conjectural, however; the only recorded appearances since the Gaskell biography are Shorter's listing[4] and a note of its sale in New York in 1915.[5] At some time after this date it came into the possession of Mrs. Symington.

The appropriate place for insertion of these tales into the Brontë canon has for a long time been marked. Half a century after Gaskell gave the world notice of the juvenile writings and reproduced a single page, Shorter prepared a chronology of the works that had come to his hand;[6] and with the publication of the Shakespeare Head edition of the Brontës' *Works*, the position of these two tales in the sequence of Charlotte's early writing was prepared in the hope that they would eventually be recovered.[7] Like minor stars plucked out from a constellation, their loss diminished but did not obscure our knowledge of the elaborate epic narrative that claimed Charlotte's imagination in her youth. Now, after more than one hundred twenty years, the first of the juvenilia to reach the public eye becomes the latest to be incorporated into our knowledge of Charlotte Brontë's work.

The Miscellaneous and Unpublished Writings of Charlotte and Patrick Branwell Brontë, vols. 8 and 9 of the Shakespeare Head edition of the Brontës' works (London, 1936–1938), 9:471–73. J. A. Symington is no relative of the American Symington family who later owned the manuscript.

4. Shorter, 2:431.

5. Mildred G. Christian, "A Census of Brontë Manuscripts in the United States," *The Trollopian* 2 (1947–1948):190. The prefatory material to this list also describes T. J. Wise's irresponsible handling of the manuscripts.

6. Shorter, 2:430–34.

7. Wise and Symington, 8:314.

CONTENTS

Alexander Jervey Esq.r M.P.
Ætat 21.

THE SECRET

AND

Lily Hart. Inscribed

by Lord

Charles

Wellesley

Verdopolis

THE SECRET

CHAPTER THE 1st

CHAPTER THE 11th

All that thy foot will see
White sunsets mournfully
Through the line gleaming

O these deep hollow tones
Sad those inspire
They like the thrilling moans
Born through lyre

Echo from rock & cave
Silently lying
And yet the howling wave
Rock the winds sighing

Far in the blank sky
wandering worlds grieve
Thus they still beam on high
Triumphed for ever

But we poor mean vision
follow like billows
Gems will be my tomb
Sea-sand my pillow

Then my embalmed corse
None shall remember
Come like the living flame
Quenched like the living ember

CHAPTER THE III.d

CHAPTER THE IVth

Dark is the mansion of the dead
Dark desolate and still
Around it dwells a solemn dread
Within a chilling chill

O mother! does thy spirit rest
In fairer worlds than ours?
'Mid ever-living valleys ever-blest
And ever blooming bowers?

I trust it does, for her pale day
Hath fixed no fairer abode
Shut from yon true happy light of day
Pressed by the cold earth's sod

Yet mother! I would rest with thee
In thy long dreamless sleep
Though freed the sweets solemnity
All voiceless, still & deep

And I would rest my weary head
Upon thy lifeless breast
Nor feel the shuddering thrill of dread
At what my temples prest

Earth is a dreary wild to me
Heaven is a cloud of gloom
Then mother! let me sleep with thee
Safe in thy chilly tomb

CHAPTER THE Ist

A dead silence had reigned in the Home Office of Verdopolis for three hours on the morning of a fine summer's day, interrupted only by such sounds as the scraping of a penknife, the dropping of a ruler, an occasional cough or whisper, and now and then some brief mandate, uttered by the noble first secretary, in his commanding tones. At length that sublime personage, after completing some score or so of despatches, addressing a small, slightly built young gentleman who occupied the chief situation among the clerks, said:

'Mr. Rhymer, will you be good enough to tell me what o'clock it is?'

'Certainly, my lord!' was the prompt reply as, springing from his seat, the ready underling, instead of consulting his watch like other people, hastened to the window in order to mark the sun's situation; having made his observations, he answered:

'Tis twelve precisely, my lord.'

'Very well', said the marquis. 'You may all give up then, and see that your desks are locked, and that not a scrap of paper is left to litter the office. Mr. Rhymer, I shall expect you to take care that my directions are fulfilled.' So saying, he assumed his hat and gloves, and with a stately tread was approaching the vestibule, when a slight bustle and whispering among the clerks arrested his steps.

'What is the matter?' asked he, turning round. 'I hope these are not sounds of contention I hear.'

'No,' said a broad, carroty-locked young man of a most pugnacious aspect, 'but—but—your lordship has forgotten that—that—'

'That what?' asked the marquis, rather impatiently.

'Oh! Merely that this afternoon is a half-holiday—and—and—'

'I understand,' replied his superior, smiling, 'you need not task your modesty with further explanation, Flannagan; the truth is, I suppose, you want your usual largess. I am obliged to you for reminding me—will that do?' he continued, as, opening his pocket-book, he took out a twenty-pound bank bill and laid it on the nearest desk.

'My lord, you are too generous', Flannagan began; but the chief secretary laughingly laid his gloved hand on his lips, and, with a condescending nod to the other clerks, sprang down the steps of the portico and strode hastily away, in order to escape the noisy expression of gratitude which now hailed his liberality.

On the opposite side of the long and wide street to that on which the splendid Home Office stands, rises the no less splendid Colonial Office; and, just as Arthur, Marquis of Douro, left the former structure, Edward Stanley Sydney departed from the latter: they met in the centre of the street.

'Well, Ned,' said my brother, as they shook hands, 'how are you to-day? I should think this bright sun and sky ought to enliven you if anything can.'

'Why, my dear Douro,' replied Mr. Sydney, with a faint smile, 'such lovely and genial weather may, and I have no doubt does, elevate the spirits of the free and healthy; but for me, whose mind and body are a continual prey to all the heaviest cares of public and private life, it signifies little whether sun cheer or rain damp the atmosphere.'

'Fudge', replied Arthur, his features at the same time assuming that disagreeable expression which my landlord denominates by the term *scorney*. 'Now don't begin to bore me, Ned, with trash of that description, I'm tired of it, quite: pray have you recollected that today is a half-holiday in all departments of the Treasury?'

'Yes; and the circumstance has cost me some money; these silly old customs ought to be abolished, in my opinion—they are ruinous.'

'Why, what have you given the poor fellows?'

'Two sovereigns.' An emphatic 'hem' formed Arthur's reply to this communication.

They had now entered Hotel Street and were proceeding in silence past the line of magnificent shops which it contains, when the sound of wheels was heard behind them and a smooth-rolling chariot dashed up and stopped just where they stood. One of the window-glasses now fell, a white hand was put out and beckoned them to draw near, while a silvery voice said, 'Mr. Sydney, Marquis of Douro, come hither a moment.'

Both the gentlemen obeyed the summons, Arthur with alacrity, Sydney with reluctance.

'What are your commands, fair ladies?' said the former, bowing respectfully to the inmates of the carriage, who were Lady Julia Sydney and Lady Maria Sneaky.

'Our commands are principally for your companion, my lord, not for you', replied the daughter of Alexander the First. 'Now Mr. Sydney', she continued, smiling on the senator, 'you must promise not to be disobedient.'

'Let me first know what I am required to perform', was the cautious answer, accompanied by a fearful glance at the shops around.

'Nothing of much consequence, Edward,' said his wife, 'but I hope you'll not refuse to oblige me this once, love. I only want a few guineas to make out the price of a pair of earrings I have just seen in Mr. Lapis's shop.'

'Not a bit of it', answered he. 'Not a farthing will I give you: it is scarce three weeks since you received your quarter's allowance, and if that is done already you may suffer for it.'

With this decisive reply, he instinctively thrust his hands into his breeches' pockets and marched off with a hurried step.

'Stingy little monkey!' exclaimed Lady Julia, sinking back on the carriage seat, while the bright flush of anger and disappointment crimsoned her fair cheek. 'This is the way he always treats me, but I'll make him suffer for it!'

'Do not discompose yourself so much, my dear', said her companion. 'My purse is at your service, if you will accept it.'

'I am sensible of your goodness, Maria, but of course I shall not take advantage of it; no, no, I can do without the earrings—it is only a fancy, though to be sure, I would rather have them.'

'My pretty cousin,' observed the marquis, who, till now, had remained a quiet though much amused spectator of the whole scene, 'you are certainly one of the most extravagant young ladies I know: why, what on earth can you possibly want with those trinkets? To my knowledge you have at least a dozen different sorts of ear-ornaments.'

'That is true, but then these are quite of another kind; they are so pretty and unique that I could not help wishing for them.'

'Well, since your heart is so much set upon the baubles, I will see whether my purse can compass their price, if you will allow me to accompany you to Mr. Lapis's.'

'Oh! thank you, Arthur, you are very kind', said Lady Julia, and both the ladies quickly made room for him as he sprang in and seated himself between them.

'I think,' said Maria Sneaky, who has a touch of the romp about her, 'I think when I marry I'll have just such a husband as you, my lord Marquis, one who won't deny me a pretty toy when I have a desire to possess it.'

'Will you?' said Arthur. 'I really think the Turks are more sensible people than ourselves.'

In a few minutes they reached the jeweller's shop. Mr. Lapis received them with an obsequious bow, and proceeded to display his glittering stores. The pendants which had so fascinated Lady Julia were in the form of two brilliant little humming-birds, whose jewelled plumage equalled if not surpassed the bright hues of nature. Whilst she was completing her purchase, a customer of a different calibre entered. This was a tall woman attired in a rather faded silk dress, a large bonnet, and a double veil of black lace which, as she lifted it on entering the shop, discovered a countenance which apparently had witnessed the vicissitudes of between thirty and forty summers. Her features might or might not have been handsome in youth, though they certainly exhibited slight traces of beauty now. On the contrary, a sharp nose, thin, blue lips, and flat eyebrows formed an assemblage of rather repulsive lineaments, even when aided by highly rouged cheeks and profusely frizzed dark locks.

One would have thought that such a person as I have described would have attracted but little attention from a young and gay nobleman like my brother. He, however, fixed his piercing eye upon her the moment she made her appearance. His gaze, nevertheless, did not indicate admiration, but rather curiosity and contempt; a keenly inquisitive expression, mingled with one of scorn, filled his countenance while he watched her.

With a slow and stiff movement she approached the counter, and addressing a shopman, desired to look at some rings. He instantly lifted the glass case and exposed to her view several hundreds of the articles she wanted. Deliberately the lady examined them all, but not one would suit. Diamonds, rubies, pearls, emeralds, topaz, etc. were each in their turn inspected and rejected. At length the shopman, who was a little out of patience at her extreme fastidiousness of choice, inquired what description of ring she could possibly want, since the first jeweller's depot in Verdopolis did not contain it.

'The ring I am in quest of', replied she, 'should be very small, of plain gold with a crystal stone, containing a little braided chestnut-coloured hair and this name (taking a scrap of paper from her reticule) engraven on the inside.'

'Well, madam,' answered he, 'we certainly have not just such an article as that in the shop at present, but we could very easily make one for you.'

'Could you finish it today?' asked she.

'Yes.'

'Then do so, and I will call for it this evening at nine o'clock.'

With these words she turned to leave the shop. Her eyes, as she lifted them from the counter, fell on the marquis and met his scrutinizing glance. For a moment she seemed to quail under its influence, but presently recovering herself, she dropped him a low curtsey, which was returned by a very slight and haughty bow, and sailed into the street.

'Who is that odd-looking woman?' asked Lady Julia as she drew on her gloves, after having finally completed her tedious bargain.

The marquis made no answer; but Maria Sneaky said, with an arch look, 'Some *ci-devant chère amie* of Douro's, I suppose; or perhaps a lady who will hereafter partake with me the benefit of a [illegible] matrimonial dispensation.'

'Is it so, Arthur?' inquired his cousin.

'Nay, Julia, I shall not tell you. You may draw your own inferences from the circumstances of the case.'

When he had assisted the ladies to their chariot, received his due tribute of parting smiles and thanks, and beheld the brilliant equipage roll merrily off, my brother turned down Hotel Street and directed his steps towards Victoria Square. A thoughtful and somewhat moody cloud darkened his brow as he entered Wellesley House, ascended the grand staircase, and proceeded through a succession of passages and chambers to the marchioness's apartment. On opening the door, and drawing aside the green damask curtain which hung within, he found her seated alone at a table and engaged in finishing a pencil sketch. She raised her head as he approached and welcomed him with a smile whose sweetness was more eloquent than words.

'Well, Marian,' said he, bending over her to look at the drawing, 'what is this you are about?'

'Only a little landscape, my lord, which I sketched in the valley yesterday.'

'It is really very pretty, and most charmingly pencilled; I think I remember the view. Is it not from the gateway of York Villa?'

'Yes, Arthur, and I have introduced Mr. Sydney in the foreground with a book in his hand.'

The marquis now sat down beside his wife and continued for some time silently watching the progress of her pencil. At length he recommenced the conversation by saying, 'Whom do you think I have seen in the city today, Marian?'

'I'm sure I don't know; perhaps Julius. I desired Mina to take him out for an airing about half an hour since.'

'No, you are far wrong in your guess.'

'Who, then?'

'None other than your old governess, Miss Foxley.'

At hearing this name, the colour faded from Marian's cheek. She paused in the midst of her employment, and slowly raising her large blue eyes from the paper, fixed them on Arthur with a look of deep alarm. He observed her agitation, and the thoughtful aspect of his countenance darkened into something like displeasure as he continued:

'What, Marian, is not that inexplicable spell yet broken? I thought absence and kind treatment might do much, but it appears all my affection has not yet succeeded in erasing that impression which, by some mysterious means, Miss Foxley contrived to make on your too sensitive mind.'

Tears now began to fill the marchioness's eyes and were dropping unheeded on her drawing as she answered, in a subdued tone, 'Do not be angry, Arthur.'

'I am not angry, Marian,' he replied, 'but can you deny that it was owing to that creature's cursed influence that you so long and steadfastly refused my hand, heart, and coronet—even when, as you have so often confessed, your inclination was not averse to the offer and when, as I could perceive, a final rejection would have blasted your happiness for life? Is it not from that cause that those transient periods of melancholy arise, with which you are even now oppressed?' Marian made no answer; he went on. 'How you at length summoned sufficient courage to throw off her shackles and consent to felicity I know not, nor is my penetration sufficiently keen to divine; but it appears there are yet some lingering remains of her power. Come, Marian, dismiss this weakness. How can she hurt you whilst under my protection? Make me your father confessor—you cannot find one more indulgent—and reveal all.'

Still there was no reply. The marquis now rose in anger. 'This is obstinacy, Marian,' he said, 'as well as weakness. I shall leave you for the present to reflect on the consequences of a continuance in such folly, but first let me warn you that I shall not suffer that woman to enter my house, or permit you to have any communication with her; and if I find my commands in this respect are disobeyed, I shall consider our interests as thenceforth separate. It is no part of my plan to allow the existence of a counteracting influence to my own in that heart and family where I ought to reign paramount.'

With these words he closed the door, and in a few minutes the echo of his retreating footsteps died away along the distant corridor.

It may perhaps be necessary to give my reader a more particular account of Miss Foxley before I proceed with my narrative. This I shall do in as few words as possible. She was the only child of a respectable merchant who died insolvent, leaving her an orphan, at the age of twenty-one, with no other fortune than her accomplishments—which were numerous—and her abilities—which, though not of the highest order, were nevertheless of a kind well fitted to enable her to push her way through the world, consisting chiefly in a capacity of discovering people's natural dispositions and adapting herself to them so as to worm a way into their good graces, and a certain sharp-sighted shrewdness wherever her own interests were concerned. In early youth she was not devoid of personal graces; but her beauty bore no proportion to her vanity, and any wound in that quarter never healed, but continued to fester till revenge in some tangible shape was achieved on the offending person. On her father's death, being unable to support herself in independence, she entered the family of the late Lady Hume in the situation of companion, and, as such, contrived so far to secure the confidence of that amiable and unsuspicious woman that on the birth of Marian she was appointed governess, for which office she was well qualified as far as talents and acquirements went. After Lady Hume's death, which took place when her daughter was fourteen years old, Miss Foxley still continued to reside at Sir Alexander's residence in Wellington's Land and was there when Arthur began to pay his addresses to her lovely young pupil. Unfortunately, the governess, who had now numbered her thirty-fifth year, was prompted by her unextinguishable vanity to imagine that she yet possessed charms potent enough to attract the admiration of a handsome and high-born nobleman. Under the influence of this delusion, she employed every art to draw away my brother's affections from the little unsophisticated girl who, in her opinion, knew not how to appreciate their value. Her efforts, however, were unsuccessful; they excited disgust instead of love; and at length, one afternoon when she was even more than usually forward, Arthur plainly though politely intimated that she was rather too old and obscure to form a fit wife for him. This was sufficient to kindle all the bad passions in Miss Foxley's mind. She vowed mentally to make him regret his cold and scornful rejection, and thenceforth set herself sedulously to work in order to prevent his union with her beautiful and youthful rival.

The effect of her endeavours soon became but too apparent. For some time Marian carefully avoided her noble lover, refused his hand, shunned his attentions, and so managed that Arthur, Marquis of Douro, the proudest and haughtiest youth of Verdopolis, was reduced to the condition of a pining, consumptive, lovesick young gentleman. Meantime, it was universally believed in the city that the delay of his union with the daughter of Sir Alexander Hume was owing to my father's opposition. How great would have been the surprise of all ranks had it been known by whom the objection was really started. It was evident, however, that Miss Hume's perseverance in this course was not unattended with pain to herself: her wan looks, attenuated form, and tearful eyes soon proclaimed that there was a wasting worm within. Still, however, she constantly refused to listen to my brother's passionate professions; and the triumph of Miss Foxley's intrigues was nearly completed when one day Arthur, having resolved to make a last attempt and then give up in despair, arrived at Badey Hall; to his astonishment he was at once shown into Marian's drawing-room, where he found her alone. What eloquent arguments he made use of to plead his cause, I know not; certain it is, however, that he was this time successful; and three weeks after, his lovely tyrant, amidst smiles, tears, and blushes, pledged her troth to him at the high altar [of St. Michael's] Cathedral. The first act of his authority as a husband was to command the immediate dismissal of Miss Foxley, who was consequently turned to the right about. He subsequently attempted to win from Marian an explanation of the causes which had so long delayed his happiness; but on this subject she maintained a mysterious silence; and he had for some time ceased to trouble her about it, till the governess's reappearance brought it again most unpleasantly to his memory.

CHAPTER THE IInd

When the marquis was gone, Marian, with a deep sigh, bent again over her half-finished picture; but now the pencil seemed to have lost its power, or the hand which directed it its skill. Instead of the flowing, correct lines and soft shadows which she had before produced, tremulous, wavering strokes and dark blotches mocked her unavailing efforts. At last she relinquished the attempt, and after replacing the sketch in her portfolio and closing the ivory box which contained her drawing materials, she drew towards her a harp which stood near. At first her slender, snowy fingers only extracted a few melancholy though sweet notes from the quivering strings; but soon these unconnected sounds gave place to a melody simple yet exquisitely plaintive; and ere long the according tones of her flutelike voice changed it to a delicious harmony while she sang the following little metrical fragment:

On the shore of the dark, wild sea,
Alone I am roaming,
While sounds its voice mournfully
Through the dim gloaming.

O! those deep, hollow tones
Sad thoughts inspire,
They swell like the thrilling moans
From breeze-swept lyre.

Echoes from rock and cave,
Solemnly dying,
Answer the howling wave,
Mock the wind's sighing.

Far in the silent sky,
Wandering worlds quiver;
Thus they shall beam on high,
Changeless for ever.

But ere another moon
Silvers the billow,
Ocean will be my tomb,
Sea-sand my pillow.

Then my unhallowed name
None shall remember:
Gone like the dying flame,
Quenched like the ember.

There were yet two verses of the fragment unsung, when she was interrupted by a rap at the door.

'Come in', said the marchioness, and Mina entered, carrying a lovely infant.

'Well, my darling', exclaimed she, as with an assumed expression of cheerfulness she rose and held out her arms to receive the pretty scion. 'How are you after your walk?'

'The fresh air has brought a little colour into his cheeks, my lady', replied Mina, relinquishing her charge.

'I see it has, and since that is the case, you had better take him out daily for the future, Mina.'

'Yes, I shall, my lady', replied the waiting-maid, seating herself at a small work-table and taking up a white robe which she previously had been embroidering for her mistress.

Marian for a few minutes continued talking to her little Julius and endeavouring to amuse him with the coral and gold bell suspended round his waist; but soon sad thoughts seemed to come over her mind, for she ceased to speak and sat gazing on the child with eyes of mournful meaning. Mina, who is a shrewd, penetrating girl, firmly attached to the marchioness and high in her confidence, presently perceived this depression of spirits, and desirous to learn the cause of it, she broke silence by saying, 'I fear something has happened to vex my lord.'

'What makes you think so?' asked Marian, starting.

'Because when I met him on the strand a little while since, he neither spoke to me nor Lord Julius, as he always does if he is in a good temper, but passed on with a grave and sorrowful look, though the little darling cried to go to him.'

To these words the marchioness made no reply, and Mina, resuming her work, continued to trace the rich pattern in silence. They continued thus employed for about half an hour, when a second rap was heard at the door. Mina rose to open it; a footman stood without with a letter.

'Who brought this, William?' asked his lady, after a hasty glance at the seal and direction.

'A little boy, my lady, who said that it had been given him by a woman in Harley Street.'

'Is he gone?'

'Yes, ma'am.'

'Very well, William, that will do.'

Hurriedly Marian broke the seal and ran over the contents of the letter. Her features whitened while she read, and at the conclusion it dropped from her nerveless hands. She would have fallen to the ground, had not the ready Mina been in an instant at her side. Happily she did not faint. On the contrary, a few minutes restored the vanishing rose to her cheek and lip. She then desired to be left alone. 'You may carry your work, Mina, into my dressing-room', said she. 'Take Julius to his nurse. Let no one come here till I ring the bell. I wish to be undisturbed for a short time.'

Mina accordingly withdrew, and it was midnight before she was again summoned to attend her lady. All the other servants had retired to rest an hour before, and she alone remained in the deserted hall, anxiously awaiting the expected sound. At length, just as she had formed the resolution to go uncalled, twelve o'clock struck and the wished-for tinkle sounded.

On opening the sitting-room door, she saw the marchioness placed exactly as she had left her, in a chair near the hearth, resting her head against the mantle-piece. There was no candle in the apartment, and in the grate the last feeble embers were just expiring.

'Will you not go upstairs now, my lady?' asked Mina. 'I have brought your bedroom lamp.'

'No, Mina, not yet. But come in, I want to speak to you.'

The waiting-maid closed the door and sat down in a chair which her mistress pointed out. Marian then continued, 'You know the marquis, Mina, as well as I do, and that being almost perfect himself, he cannot brook imperfection in others. His word and command have hitherto been my law, to which I have always submitted myself with cheerfulness and pleasure. Tonight, however, I am going to set in direct opposition to his will. Utter necessity must plead my excuse for such otherwise unpardonable disobedience; but if he discovers it, I am lost. Do you know where Harley Street is, Mina? I must go there this night.'

'No, my lady, I do not; but surely you do not intend to go alone?'

'Yes, I do.'

'That cannot be, my lady. You would be lost in the city. Do let my father go with you; he knows every street and lane of Verdopolis.'

'Is he in the house?'

'Yes, my lord ordered him to sleep here every night.'

'Call him, then.'

Mina left the room and in about ten minutes returned accompanied by her father.

Ned halted at the door for a moment. 'Come in, Edward', said the marchioness in her sweet, mild tone.

'I was only stripping my shoes, my lady,' said he, 'cause they're not fit to walk on such a grand carpet as this.'

'Oh, never mind that', replied she with a faint smile at his punctilious decorum. 'I am sorry to have called you from your bed, Edward, but I wished to learn from you what quarter of the city Harley Street is situated in.'

'Harley Street? Why, it's the same as they call Paradise Street, my lady, 'cause there's a house in it that you wouldn't like to pass by yourself at this time of night.'

'Should I not? Then will you go with me?'

'That I will, with all the pleasure in life.'

'Fetch my hat and cloak, then, Mina.'

'Had you not better take mine, my lady?' asked the prudent *fille de chambre*.

'Yes, on second thought that would certainly be the best.'

Mina again left the room and shortly came back with a plain straw hat and brown silk mantle. In these she attired her young mistress, and then, after lighting the fair adventurer and her guide down a private staircase to a street door, of which she possessed the key, returned to the servants' hall, and stretching herself on a [chintz] sofa that stood at the side of the still blazing hearth, was soon buried in a profound sleep.

The night was wild and stormy; vast, billowy clouds, from which a drizzling rain incessantly distilled, rolled over the sky, and at times, as they parted their folds, the serene moon was revealed shining far beyond them. A chill north wind mingled its moaning with that of the troubled sea, whose howling waves might now be heard uttering their voice afar off. With a light step and beating heart, Marian trod the wet, gloomy streets, preceded by her trusty conductor. After passing through many wide squares and long, broad streets, they entered a dark lane which would scarcely admit more than four persons abreast. On one side a line of lofty buildings arose, in the centre of which a sudden burst of moonlight discovered a flight of steps surmounted by a portico.

'This is Harley Street, my lady', said Ned, stopping and turning [illegible] around.

'Is it, Edward?' replied she in a low tone; and then, as if seized with a sudden agitation, she sank on the steps before mentioned.

Scarcely had she sat there for five minutes, when the sound of many footsteps was heard approaching. All was now again dark, so that nothing could be distinguished; but as the persons drew near, Marian easily recognized several by their voices.

'I think, vice-president, we are late tonight', said one in a deep, calm tone.

'Yes, most worthy [illegible]', was the reply, uttered in a voice which struck chill dismay to the marchioness's heart and caused her instantly to take refuge behind a sort of projecting pillar. 'Yes, we are, and I'll wager ten to one that Gordon proposes to fine us for it.'

'Taken, my lord Marquis', exclaimed another.

'Is that O'Connor?' asked the former speaker.

'Yes.'

'Done, then, and I hope to fleece you well, my most excellent knight of the mattock.'

Here the door within the vestibule opened and a sudden glare of lamps streamed on the dense, dark night, revealing the forms of about twenty of thirty gentlemen, most of them tall handsome men.

> Pride in their port, defiance in their eye,
> These mighty lords of human-kind passed by.*

Tumultuously they sprang or rushed up the steps into a vast and magnifi-

---

* Cf. Oliver Goldsmith, *The Traveller*: "Pride in their port, defiance in their eye,/I see the lords of human kind pass by" (ll. 327–28).

cent hall, blazing with sunlike chandeliers which appeared above. Then the door closed and night reassumed her solemn, silent reign.

'Those are rare young chaps', said Ned, as he rejoined the terrified marchioness. 'If they had seen you, there would have been some'at to do; only his lordship was there, and that would have [illegible] checked them a bit, I guess.'

'Let us proceed now, Edward', said she.

'Which house are we to stop at, my lady?'

'The last in the street, on the left hand.'

They soon reached it, and Marian, after directing Ned to wait on the outside till she should return, knocked timidly at the door. It was presently opened by a dirty-looking servant wench in a dingy lace cap and gaudy cotton gown.

'Is there not a lady of the name of Miss Foxley lodging here?' asked the marchioness.

'Yes, madam, and if you'll follow me I'll show you her apartment.' Accordingly, after carefully fastening the door, she led the way up a narrow flight of stone steps and through a sort of lobby, which was dimly lighted by a single lamp, to a room at the further end. Entering first, she announced that the lady was come.

'Indeed', said someone within; 'bring her here directly'; and the visitor was ushered into a small chamber, whose furniture consisted of a mahogany pembroke table, five or six cane-bottomed chairs, a scanty carpet, faded green window curtains, and a broken paper screen. A small but bright fire burned in the grate, and beside it a tall female was seated in an armchair. She rose as Marian entered and advanced to meet her, saying, 'My lady Marchioness, how are you? I am surprised at your condescension in deigning to visit so obscure an individual as myself. Pray be seated, if these poor chairs are not too mean to support a peeress of the realm '

'Miss Foxley,' replied the marchioness, as she took the offered seat, 'I have run considerable risk in complying with your request; nor am I sure that my conduct in this respect is right; but my anxiety to learn the truth of what your letter hinted at induced me to disregard all other considerations. Pray give me a more explicit account without delay.'

'Why, madam!' returned the governess, with a fiendlike smile. 'You are doubtless now a happy wife, loving and beloved. The marquis, by all accounts, makes a fond husband; and a son, I understand, has lately crowned your felicity. But, my lady, is not this bliss too perfect to endure?

Do you not dread an interruption? A profound calm is generally succeeded by a storm. Do you not know of one whose appearance would utterly blast all this course of ecstatic pleasure?'

'Miss Foxley, Miss Foxley,' murmured Marian, in a scarcely audible tone, 'don't torture me so, for heaven's, for my mother's sake, whom you once respected. End this suspense and let me know the worst. Is he returned?'

'I will show you', answered Miss Foxley, ringing the bell, which was almost instantly answered by the servant-maid. 'Tell the gentleman in the next room I wish to speak with him', said she.

The girl departed, and almost immediately after a young man entered the room. He was tall and genteelly formed, with brown hair, wild dark eyes, and a handsome though meagre countenance.

'Mr. Henry,' said Miss Foxley, 'allow me to introduce your early friend, Marian Hume, to you. [Now,] unfortunately, she bears another surname, but that is not my fault.'

He approached the marchioness, who sat with her face buried in her hands, and said, 'Madam, permit me to announce myself as that long-absent Henry Percy, who once, at least, was honoured with your regard.'

At the sound of his voice, she raised her head, looked at him fixedly for some minutes, and then replied, 'This is not, cannot be Henry. He was younger, fairer, his voice softer. Miss Foxley, you are deceiving me; this person scarcely resembles him in the least.'

'That may be', answered the governess, 'yet, notwithstanding, he is Henry Percy, your Henry Percy, and no other.'

'I deny it, here is his picture (taking a portrait from her bosom). Compare them and tell me where the similitude lies.'

'Madam,' interposed the young man, 'I do not wonder at your denial of my identity. The lapse of time and a long sojourn in foreign climates must necessarily have produced a vast change; but though I may be altered externally, yet within all is as it ever was, which is, I fear, more than can be said of some other.'

'Do not insult me, sir', said Marian, the deadly white to which her cheek had faded giving place to a bright flush of anger. 'I shall believe the evidence of my senses, rather than your assertions.'

'Since you will not credit my word,' replied he, 'look at this token, and reject its testimony if you dare.'

So saying, he put into her hand a small silver box. She opened it: a single glance at its contents seemed to bring sudden and forcible conviction; for with a faint shriek she sank back in the chair, almost deprived of animation.

'Now, perjured one, do you acknowledge me?' asked Mr. Percy with bitter emphasis.

'I do, I do, but oh! spare me for one week: give me at least that time for thought, for consideration.'

'Not a day, not an hour will I spare you! My claim is legal and I will enforce it now.'

The marchioness then fell on her knees, and with streaming eyes and clasped hands implored a reprieve, however short. Her extreme agony seemed at length to move him.

'Rise, madam', said he. 'You shall have a week's delay, on condition that you promise not to consult with the Marquis of Douro during that time.'

'And', added Miss Foxley, 'on condition that you likewise promise to return here tomorrow night in order to receive important information respecting yourself, my lady, which you do not at present appear to be in a situation to listen to.'

'I will promise anything!' exclaimed she, grateful for this temporary relief. 'But of what nature is the information you allude to, Miss Foxley?'

'I merely wish to let you know who and what you are, a circumstance of which you have hitherto been ignorant.'

'Cannot I hear it now?'

'No, it is too late, and the dawn is already rising.'

Marian, then, after some further conversation, took her leave. She found Ned anxiously awaiting her return in the street by the dim light of the breaking day. They hastily trod the path to Wellesley House, where, fortunately, they arrived unobserved. Ned, then, after receiving his young lady's cordial thanks, which he valued even more than the solid reward which accompanied them, retired to enjoy in peace the refreshment of undisturbed slumber. The marchioness likewise sought her pillow; but sorrow and sad thought banished sleep far from the stately couch where she lay.

CHAPTER THE IIIrd

On the night after that spoken of in my last chapter, the drawing-room at Ellrington House exhibited a more tranquil scene than it usually does. Instead of the dark political [design], turbulent and boisterous wine party, or [dazzling and bewildering] crowd of Fashion's bright devotées, two persons alone, the lord and lady of the mansion, sat one on each side of the cheerful and tranquil hearth. A few wax tapers on the mantel piece, shining amongst a hundred sparkling decorations aided by the blaze of a clear fire, furnished light sufficient to enable Lord Ellrington to peruse a treatise on the present state of society, and his wife to decipher the characters of a Persian poem. At length the former, after several muttered expressions of contempt for his author, threw down the work and said, 'Come, Zenobia, give up poring over that absurd [passion] you are at there. I dare say, if one could read it, it's the rarest trash in nature.'

'Indeed, Ellrington, you are mistaken; finer sentiments were never embodied in language. But what book have you been reading all this time?'

'A translation into the English tongue of an ass's bray.'

'Indeed? Then you were less profitably employed than myself. I was construing the song of a nightingale to his favourite rose.'

'And pray, what is the name of the idiot who has conceived that surpassingly magnificent idea?'

'[Ferdoona], one of the greatest poets Persia ever produced.'

'And do you really, Zenobia, admire such groveling nonsense?'

'Most undoubtedly I do.'

'Well, women are the most incomprehensible creatures on earth; sometimes you seem to be possessed of considerable sense and discernment, and then again you commit acts and utter speeches which argue a great weakness, if not a total deprivation, of intellect.'

'Granting it is so, Alexander: might I not say the same of you? How often during the revolution of a year are you as rational as at present?'

'If I were not in a particularly easy humour tonight that sentence would stick in my throat, Zenny.'

'Would it? And most likely, in that case, a bottle of wine would be necessary to wash it down.'

'Probably, but tell me, now I think on it, what makes you hide all your hair under that singularly formed cap which you have lately worn?'

'Fashion, my lord, and the caprice of custom.'

'What? Does Fashion induce the ladies to destroy their beauty?'

'Sometimes, but since you dislike it, the defect is easily remedied.' So saying, she plucked out the comb which confined her hair, and immediately a cloud of raven tresses fell down in rich profusion over her neck and shoulders.

'There,' said Ellrington after a moment's silence, 'you look like yourself, now. It is astonishing what a difference the presence or absence of a few curled locks makes.'

Pleased with her attention to his wishes, he found himself in a better and more amicable humour than any which had soothed his stormy soul for many a long year, when, just as he had reached the acme of suavity, a rap was heard at the door.

'Come in', said he, and the servant who stood without was startled at the gentleness of tone in which these words were pronounced, as generally, when he ventured to disturb his master thus, a volley of oaths and curses formed the reward of his pains. Timidly opening the door, he announced that a person wished to speak with Lord Ellrington.

'A person! And pray, what kind of a one is it, coming here at this time of night?'

'It is a woman, my lord, and, I believe, a young one, though she keeps her face so covered with a handkerchief that I can't see it distinctly.'

'Hey! some mystery! Well, show her into the library and say I'll come directly.'

'What can the creature possibly want?' said Lady Zenobia. 'I think, Ellrington, it was foolish of you not to send a denial.'

'Oh! nonsense, Zenny. She may have something particular to tell me, you know.'

When Lord Ellrington entered the library, he perceived a slender female figure attired in a silk mantle and a large straw hat which had fallen back and discovered a luxuriant flow of beautiful chestnut ringlets. Her face was turned away and partially hidden with the palms of her small white hands.

'Well, my girl,' said he, 'what is your business with me?'

At first she made no answer. He repeated the question. She then slowly lifted her head and discovered a countenance which, bright with blushes and formed in the most exquisite mould of youthful loveliness, appeared an object so fair and fascinating that the lofty nobleman could not restrain an exclamation of surprise. After gazing at her a moment with an astonished air, he said, 'Do I deceive myself, or is this the peerless Marchioness of Douro?'

'My lord, your conjecture is right', replied she, at once seeming to throw off the bashfulness which had before oppressed her and fearlessly meeting his fixed gaze with an eye that sparkled almost with the light of insanity. 'I am that unhappy woman.'

'And to what am I indebted for this unexpected, though most welcome, pleasure?'

'To desperation, my lord. Nothing short of that should have made me humble myself so.'

'I am sorry for that, fair lady, as I hoped you were come of free will; but tell me, in what I can serve you? It shall not be said that the prettiest woman in Verdopolis asked my assistance in vain.'

'Do not talk so, Lord Ellrington', exclaimed Marian, while a sudden shudder ran through her whole frame. 'Knowing what I know, such light language sounds horrible.'

'And what do you know, my lady?'

'What I would not tell you for worlds and what I am come here in order to confirm, though I fear it scarce needs confirmation.'

'This is mysterious language, I do not understand it.'

'But you will ere long. Tell me, my lord, have you not a casket belonging to the late Lady Percy, which up to this day you have never been able to open?'

'I have, but how in the name of the heavens, the earth, the seas, and all that are therein did you obtain knowledge of it?'

'That I cannot explain to you at present, my lord. Permit me only to see the box, and I will show you a method of opening it.'

'Well, I really cannot refuse a request from such lips, so permit me, my lady Marchioness, to conduct you into the apartment where the object of your curiosity is kept.' With these words, he offered to take her hand. She, however, withdrew it with an apparently involuntary movement of repulsion.

'What?' said he, scowling furiously, 'do you dare to reject in disdain that courtesy which it was almost a condescension for me to offer?'

'I was wrong', replied Marian, bursting into tears. 'You may take my hand, Lord Ellrington, for I fear you have a right to command me in everything.'

The last words were uttered in so low a tone as to be inaudible to his lordship. Her tears, however, softened him, as he imagined them to arise from a dread of his anger. He therefore accepted the hand which otherwise might perhaps now have been declined, and taking up a candle, led her out of the room.

They passed in silence across the entrance hall, ascended the grand staircase, and trod with noiseless step the matted floor of a long gallery, at the termination of which was a door. This Lord Ellrington unlocked, and they entered a small apartment panelled with black oak. In the centre of it stood a table covered with papers and in one corner an elaborately carved cabinet in which lay four swords, three sheathed and one naked. Above them hung a large banner, blood-red and bearing for its device a skull and cross-bones in black.

'This', said the nobleman, after having again locked the door, 'is my *sanctum sanctorum*, lady Marchioness.' He paused and looked steadily upon her, as if to see what impression the scene produced.

It was indeed a strangely awful situation for poor Marian to be placed in. There she stood at the dead hour of the night, alone and face to face with that dark, stern man whose mighty talents and still mightier crimes will hereafter appall the muse of history as she records them. A deep and boding silence reigned around, interrupted only by the faint, dull sound of a closing door [or] hurried tread from some distant part of the vast mansion, sounds that only served to intimate that help, if needed, was too far off to be obtained. Cold ran the blood to that youthful lady's heart as she thought on these things, but terror so restrained her tongue and fettered her limbs while under the influence of that searching falcon eye, that she neither breathed a word nor moved a finger.

'How do you like it?' he continued with a sardonic smile, lifting the lamp and drawing up his lofty form to all its majestic height. 'You see those four swords and that red flag on the cabinet yonder?'

She bowed.

'Well, now, my lady, I'll tell you what they mean. This is the blade I wielded in my youth, when I killed Negroes for Wellington. This is the weapon that helped me in exile; it is drunk with the blood of merchants by sea and land. And [this] not many years since, made Alexander the First tremble on his mountain throne. Those three are all sheathed; they have done their work, they have slain their thousand and tens of thousands and now they may rest. But for this other! Look at it, my lady, look at it well. See how sharp and bright and glittering it is—not a spot of blood, not a streak of rust blackens it. This is a virgin sword, it has pierced no heart, freed no spirit; but it lies bare and ready; it bides its time. A voice and a power is in that weapon: the voice shall speak the doom of nations; the power shall execute it. And by the strength of what arm shall it do these things?' he continued, suddenly laying his hand on her shoulder with a force that made her tremble. 'And for what prize will the great game be played? Mine is the arm, a crown is the prize!'

He paused a moment, and then went on again in a lower tone. 'As for that flag, it is the pennon of the Black Rover. For seven years it swept the seas, the dreaded, the invincible. In storm and sunshine, war and mirth, the battle and the festival, she remained unhurt, unchanged. When the waves were strewed with the tempest-torn fragments of the merchantman and the man-of-war, my good ship, their dread and scourge, spread her white sail and, like a haunting spirit of the deep, proudly breasted those waters that none else dared look upon. Men said she was charmed against wind and wave, and they spoke truth; for I trod her deck and directed her course, therefore Destiny with her triple shield ever hovered round—

'But stop! Am I a madman or an idiot, to talk thus to you? Humph! I fear I have been letting out. But it is easy to prevent consequences. Kneel down, my Marchioness of Douro, kneel this instant. Dare you resist? There, that is right. You must excuse the push I gave you, but it is always best to obey me at once without hesitation. Now swear by the head of that old man whom you worship never to whisper in mortal ear one word of what I have been saying this night. Swear, or—'

'I do swear', said she in a faint voice.

'That is well. Get up. You are an obedient and praiseworthy girl, and if I had the management of you would soon arrive at the perfection of feminine meekness and humility.'

Marian rose and stood before the imperious nobleman. She was deadly pale and might have passed for a beautiful marble statue, had not the tremor which shook every limb indicated that her form was of living flesh and blood. Lord Ellrington again fixed his eye on her and seemed to take pleasure in witnessing the profound awe which his keen gaze inspired. At last, after torturing her thus for some minutes, he broke out into a long and loud burst of laughter. She stepped back and looked at him doubtingly, as if she thought his brain disturbed.

'Well,' he exclaimed as soon as the exhaustion arising from his strange fit of merriment would permit him to speak, 'have I frightened you, my lady? Come! nonsense! cheer up! One would think you were never spoken to harshly or looked at sternly before. Pray, does the marquis never discipline you a little in this way? Confess the truth now, is he not sometimes rather crusty and overbearing?'

'My lord,' stated Marian, while an indignant blush crimsoned her snowy brow and faded cheek, 'I will not hear my husband's name mentioned thus, even by you, satanically proud as you are—' She would have said more, but the half-formed words died away on her lips, and with them the transient flash of spirit likewise vanished.

'Satanically proud', muttered Lord Ellrington after her. 'That is daring. You forget, I think, my lady, where you are and how situated; but methinks you need not pretend to be so thin-skinned as it regards the marquis at the moment when you are committing what in his eyes would unquestionably appear a most deadly offence; for I do not think he is acquainted with this midnight visit to Ellrington House.'

Marian made no reply to this cutting remark; she only sighed deeply. A pause now ensued, during which Lord Ellrington slowly paced the room. It was some time before she ventured to interrupt him by again referring to the business which had occasioned her visit. At length, summoning resolution, she said hesitatingly, 'Can your lordship permit me to look at the casket now?'

Without answering, he strode directly to the cabinet and, taking a key from his pocket, unlocked it. A multitude of miscellaneous articles were contained in the different divisions; but in one, more carefully arranged than the rest, there appeared an ivory box inlaid with silver, a long braided lock of beautiful light-brown hair, a lady's watch, and a miniature portrait of a beautiful woman set in a massive gold frame, richly decorated with jewels. He took the box and put it into her hand.

She moved a few paces from him towards the table on which the lamp was placed, and having opened the casket by means of a secret spring, took from it a paper that formed the whole of its contents. This she glanced hastily over, and then, suddenly and before Lord Ellrington could prevent her, consumed it in the flame of the lamp, exclaiming when she had done, 'Thank God that evidence is destroyed.'

'How dare you?' said he, approaching her with angry strides and laying his hand, as if by instinct, on a pistol which appeared half-hidden in his breast. 'If you were a man I'd blow you to atoms for that action this moment.'

'Do it now', said Marian, perfectly undaunted by his manner, 'and rid me of a life which I have lost the power of enjoying.'

'No,' he replied, thrusting back the pistol, 'I'll not kill you, but I'll do what perhaps in your present state of mind would be almost as bad. I'll keep you locked up here till you tell me, and that truly, the contents of the paper which you have just destroyed.'

'That I will never do; every fresh view which I obtain of your conduct determines me more against it.'

'Is the silly girl mad?' said Lord Ellrington with a gloomy frown. 'Has she forgotten who and what I am?'

'No, my lord, I have not; but the sentiments which I cannot help entertaining against you will force their way despite of all my efforts to restrain them.'

'[Note], then, you may take the consequences of your want of self-government, and continue here with me at least till the morning light. If you behave well during the next five or six hours, I may perhaps permit you to return home in [time] to explain your absence to the marquis as you best can.'

In vain did Marian endeavour by entreaties, remonstrances, and even tears, to turn him from his purpose. He was inexorable; and during the remainder of that night, she was compelled to continue an unwilling prisoner, listening to the keen taunts, false insinuations, and detested gallantry of her stern jailer. At last, just as the lamp was beginning to wane before the first pale beams of dawn which shone faintly through the single lofty and narrow window with which the apartment was lighted, a hesitating knock was heard at the door.

'Who's there?' thundered Lord Ellrington.

'It is only I', replied the voice of his wife, in very subdued tones. 'I wished to know, Alexander, whether you intended to retire to rest at all before morning or not.'

'And how dare you wish to know anything about the matter? Off to your bed this instant, without reply!' Zenobia understood the accent in which her husband spoke and withdrew immediately.

'Now,' said he, turning to the marchioness, 'I will allow your little ladyship to depart. Come along.'

Gladly she followed him as, after unlocking the door, he led the way through gallery, hall, and passage to the grand entrance. This he unfastened with his own hands. Marian did not wait for any farewell ceremonies, but darting past him, cleared the steps at a spring, fled down the street with the speed and lightness of a roe, and was out of sight in a twinkling. An effusion of golden light filled the east before she reached Wellesley House. All, however, was still silent around that lordly mansion; and when she rung the bell at the private door it was opened by Mina.

'Oh, my lady,' exclaimed that faithful handmaiden, 'I am so glad you are come. I have passed such a night of suspense and misery on your account as no one ever did before, scarcely.'

'Did the marquis return home last night?' asked her mistress.

'Yes, he did at four o'clock. I then thought that your absence could not miss being discovered and gave up all for lost; but most fortunately he went to his own bedroom, and therefore everything is still safe, you know, my lady.'

'Thank Heaven and the Great Genii* who watched over me!' ejaculated the marchioness. 'Now, Mina, go to bed, as I am sure you must be tired. I can undress myself.'

---

* The Genii were the four Brontë children. Cf. Wise and Symington, 8:61.

Mina then left the room, and in a few minutes her young mistress, oppressed with grief and watching, was enjoying a temporary oblivion of her sorrows in the repose of sleep.

CHAPTER THE IVth

She had scarcely rested three hours when Mina again stood by her bedside. 'My lady,' said she, 'will you rise now? The marquis has sent up to say that breakfast is waiting.'

'What o'clock is it?' asked Marian.

'Nine, my lady.'

'Oh! then I will rise, of course. How provoking that he should have to wait for me!'

The marchioness was soon dressed, as her attire in the morning is dictated by the very spirit of tasteful simplicity; and a few touches brought her soft, naturally curling glossy tresses into becoming order. When the business of the toilette was over, she proceeded to attend the marquis. Her heart beat fast as she approached the breakfast-room, for she had not seen him since the interview mentioned in one of my former chapters, when he left her in anger, sternly prohibiting any intercourse with Miss Foxley—and how had this prohibition been attended to?

Arthur, as she entered the apartment, was seated with his back to the door, engaged in the perusal of a newspaper. Her tread was too light to attract attention; and she feared to address him unspoken to, uncertain whether he had yet forgotten his wrathful mood; so she quietly took her seat at the table and began to arrange the material for breakfast.

The tinkle of porcelain and silver soon roused him; he looked up with a smile and said, 'Well, Marian, won't you bid me good morning? I hope you are not in a bad temper at being called out of your bed so early.'

'No, indeed, Arthur, on the contrary. I am ashamed of myself for having made you wait so long. Forgive me, however, as I am not often so deficient in punctuality.'

'I'll consider about [it]', replied he playfully. 'Perhaps your request may be granted, for I do not find myself inclined to be very angry on that score.'

My brother's breakfast is generally protracted to the space of about an hour and a half, as instead of eating straightforward, like other people, he sits maundering over the morning papers and, as my landlord says, taking a sup and a bite at intervals of about a quarter of an hour each. Some ladies of my acquaintance would raise a fine hubbub if they had to wait for their husbands such an unconscionable length of time; but the Marchioness of Douro, who considers herself honoured in being permitted to attend the beck of her lord and master when she has finished her own slight repast, usually takes up some piece of ornamental fancy-work and continues patiently plying the needle with her small, slight fingers until the last leading article of the last newspaper is concluded.

This morning, her labour was interrupted by frequent and deep sighs. Every time one of these indications of grief escaped her lips, the marquis, though unseen by his wife, just lifted his eyes from the paper and surveyed her with a most peculiar expression; and when they fell again on the speech or paragraph, he seemed for a moment rather engaged with his own thoughts than the sense of what he was reading. At length, like all sub-lunary things, Arthur's breakfast had an end; the service being cleared away and all set to rights by an attendant footman, Marian was about to leave the room in order to visit her nursery, when suddenly the marquis rose, and coming close up to her, took her hand.

'Marian,' said he after a momentary silence, 'you look very pale this morning. What is the reason of it?'

'I—I—did not sleep very well last night', stammered she, while her frame trembled like an aspen leaf.

'That is not all, it could not occasion this tremor. And what makes your hand turn so cold within mine?'

'I am sure I do not know', replied Marian, endeavouring to force a smile; but the attempt only brought a tear into her dark blue eye.

The marquis looked at her as if he would have pierced to the farthest recesses of her heart, and said in a low thrilling voice, 'Have you disobeyed my mandates? Have you seen that woman and are her chains again riveted round you?'

There was a pause. Marian seemed almost annihilated; the rapidly varying hue of her countenance proclaimed the violence of those emotions with which her soul was now rent. She could not answer, she could not even look up at her imperious lord, but stood voiceless and motionless like one petrified.

'It is well', said he, dropping her hand and sternly folding his arms. 'I understand that silence. You have chosen to follow the direction of your own weak inclinations and to disregard my wishes. I have told you before that the consequence of such a line of conduct would be an immediate separation. It is my custom to make my words and deeds conformable; therefore, this very day and before three hours elapse, the travelling-carriage will be in readiness to take you to my father's countryhouse in Wellington's Land. Good-bye. This is in all probability our last interview, for I cannot love a disobedient wife.'

'Arthur, my dearest Arthur, don't leave me thus! You would not think so hardly of me if you knew all!'

'Tell me all, then!' said he hastily, and taking his hand from the door-lock, which he was just about to turn.

'I dare not!'

'And why?'

'Because I am bound by a promise not to consult you for a week; and at the end of that time all consultation will, I fear, be in vain, for then I must leave you for ever.'

The marquis was going to answer, when the door opened and his Grace the Duke of Wellington entered. He halted, as Bobadil* would say, on the threshold, and after looking keenly from Arthur to Marian and noting the attitude and countenance of each, said in a quiet tone of inquiry, 'What ails you both? Have I arrived just in time to witness a slight specimen of matrimonial felicity, eh?'

There was no answer; the marquis only moved away to a window and began to watch the clouds as they sailed slowly by. His Grace then addressed himself more particularly to the lady. 'What have you done, Marian,' said he, 'to bring that lowering and tempestuous cloud over your husband's countenance?'

Marian burst into tears. 'I did not mean to offend him', sobbed she, 'but—but—'

'What, love? I trust this is not unnecessary severity on his part.'

'No, no, no, he only wishes to know something which I cannot tell him.'

'And what is that something? Can you tell me?'

'Yes', said the marchioness, looking up, while a smile began to illumine her still glistening eyes. 'I think I will. Your Grace will know how to advise me better than anyone else, and I have not promised to keep it a secret from you.'

'Come then, child; sit down by me and let us hear this wonderful secret.'

Marian sat down beside the duke as he desired her; for a little while she was silent and seemed to be collecting her faculties and summoning resolution for some great effort. The composure of resignation rather than

---

* The allusion is not clear, but the name occurs also in Branwell's "Letters from an Englishman", Wise and Symington, 8:102. Cf. Captain Bobadil in Ben Jonson's *Every Man in his Humour*.

peace at length overspread her features, but there was still a wildness in her look and a tremble in her voice as she said, 'My lord Duke, I am not your son's wife, I am not Sir Alexander Hume's daughter.'

At these words the Marquis of Douro started as if he had received a shock of electricity. He turned round and would have spoken, but his father restrained him, saying, 'Hush, Arthur, not a word from your lips or I shall desire you to quit the room instantly. Now my love,' he continued, addressing Marian, 'explain to me in the first place how you are not my son's wife.'

'About five years ago,' replied she, 'a short time before my mother, or her whom until lately I considered as such, died, and when she was fast wasting under that languishing disease which at length destroyed her, I was one day summoned to her chamber. She was sitting up supported by pillows, and near the bedside stood Mr. Hall, our private chaplain, Miss Foxley, my governess, whom your Grace may perhaps remember to have seen (the duke nodded assent) and Henry Percy, the youngest son of Lord Ellrington, whose country-seat was situated not far from Badey Hall. He was a boy about my own age, and had been my playfellow as long as I could remember.

'"Marian," said my mother when I came to her, "you have often heard me speak of the late Lady Percy, have you not?" I said I had, and she went on, "She was my dearest friend. All her wishes are now sacred to me, and there is one of them which this day I desire to see fulfilled. On her deathbed, shortly after you and Henry were born, she expressed a wish that, in remembrance of our friendship, you should be united in case of your both arriving at years of discretion. I am now dying, and tomorrow Henry will depart on a voyage to a distant part of the world, whence he may never return. I should like, therefore, to see you betrothed now in my presence, and if my always hitherto dutiful daughter would render her mother's last moments happy, she will consent to bestow her hand on one who I doubt not will hereafter render her a happy wife."

'I could not refuse to comply with my dear mother's request, when I knew how soon the grave and coffin were to hide her forever from my sight; and besides, even had the powerful motive of obedience to her been absent, I could have found no excuse in my own inclinations to sanction a refusal: though I did not then know what love was, yet I had always liked Henry Percy, who was a handsome and affectionate boy, for his good nature and kind disposition. We accordingly pledged our faith before the chaplain and each gave the other a token by which, when we met again at some future period, we might recognize each other. The next day he set out on his long journey, and a few weeks after my mother was carried to the tomb.

'Time passed on, and I heard nothing of Henry till the third year after his departure, when one morning Miss Foxley was looking over a newspaper in which she showed me a paragraph announcing the wreck of *The Mermaid*, the ship which Henry had sailed in, among some distant and unknown countries called the South Sea Islands, and the destruction of all her crew, including Lieutenant Percy, son of the celebrated Alexander Rogue. I mourned for Henry's death, but neither long nor bitterly. Absence had caused his image and the calm, childlike affection with which I viewed him to grow dim in my mind and memory.

'Twelve months after, I saw the marquis; new feelings, passions which I had never till then experienced, arose in my heart. I need not tell your Grace that all things were settled for my union with your son, when, in what must have appeared to you an unaccountably capricious manner, I suddenly stopped the preparations and declared that I never could consent to be his wife. I had, however, a reason, and one sufficiently conclusive. Three days before my marriage was to have taken [place], and while Miss Foxley was engaged in making my bridal dress, she received a letter from a shipmate of Henry's with whom she was acquainted, declaring that the story of *The Mermaid*'s wreck was all false and that both vessel and crew were well and pursuing a prosperous voyage.

'You cannot, my lord, I think blame me if after this, though with the greatest violence to my own feelings, I broke off all intercourse with your son. None can tell what I suffered when I saw him day by day pining for my sake, but Duty strongly pointed out to me the path which I ought to pursue, and I dared not turn aside. Your opinion of my caprice must have been confirmed, when after several months of steady rejection, I at once and suddenly yielded to his entreaties. There was a cause for this, but I scarcely dare tell it you lest you should suspect me of an inclination for romance.'

The duke encouraged her to continue, and she went on. 'Late one calm summer's evening, I wandered out to a distant part of the grounds, and sitting down in a little wild alcove which was my favourite retreat, began sorrowfully to brood over the image of Arthur and the sad certainty that I should never be his. I thought and wept till it began to grow dark; and then, fearful of passing through the park at night and disturbing the deer and wild cattle from their slumbers, I rose to return and had advanced a little way up the forest walk where the alcove was erected, when a voice, faint and mournful, whispered my name. I turned and saw, standing under the arch I had just left, the dim figure of a man.

'"Who is there?" I asked in some alarm.

'Instead of answering, he glided towards me. I shrieked out. He beckoned me to be silent and said, in very hollow tones which I shudder even now to recollect, "Look at me, Marian, and know your Henry."

'Just then the moon broke from a cloud, and her light, falling through the branches, revealed to me a form and face which bore, indeed, a slight resemblance to Henry; but it was so changed and distorted that I should never have recognized it of my own accord. The hair and clothes were all wet and dripping, the eyes wide open but void of all expression save one of ghastliness, the face blue and livid and all the features swollen. I was too much appalled at this horrid change to answer, and he [went on]:

'"So I lie, Marian, among the Coral Islands of the South Sea. Listen not to deceivers, fear not that I shall return. Death and the waters of a vast deep chain me to my place; be happy and think of your first love no more." The wraith then walked into air before me, and filled with horror, I hastened back to the house.

'On arriving there, I related what I had seen to Miss Foxley. She strongly endeavoured to persuade me that it was all the fruit of my own excited imagination; but, finding my belief in the reality of the apparition fixed, and likewise my determination to act according to its counsel, she grew angry and left me, saying she prayed that if I did marry the marquis, my repentance hereafter would be deep and bitter. Three weeks subsequent to this I was married. Arthur, shortly after our union, dismissed Miss Foxley, which I was very glad of, as her sullen looks and threatening [scowls] filled me with an undefined feeling of fear.

'Since that time I have received no intelligence of her till about two days ago, when the marquis informed me that he had seen her in the city and warned me against holding any communication with her. The same day a letter was brought me from her, saying that if I did not wish the whole of a certain transaction to come out, I would condescend, marchioness as I was, to visit my old governess at her lodgings in Harley Street. I went, for I dared not do otherwise, and there I saw that Henry Percy whom till then I had supposed buried in the sea.

'He was so changed, and looked so dark and wild and meagre, that at first I denied his identity; but I was soon but too well convinced by the production of that very token which five years since I had given him as a pledge of my eternal faith. He would have claimed his right over me that instant; by tears and entreaties I, however, gained a reprieve of a week, on condition that during that time I would not consult with my husband on the subject and that I would return to Harley Street next day in order to learn an important secret concerning myself.

'At the second interview, Miss Foxley informed me that I was not the daughter of Sir Alexander Hume!

'"Who, then?" I asked.

'"The late Ladies Hume and Percy", she replied, "were, as you know, most intimate friends. As a sign of their love for and confidence in each other, they agreed, when you and Henry were born, to exchange children and each bring up the other's child as their own. The affair was managed so dexterously that none but myself knew anything of it; and till this moment you have looked up to Dr. Hume as your father, when in reality no less a person than Lord Ellrington stands in that relation to you."

'This information affected me so deeply that I fainted. On recovering, I told Miss Foxley that, unless she could bring proof of her assertion, I should consider all I had just heard in the light of a malignant falsehood. She then informed me that there was a written agreement of the affair enclosed in a casket of Lady Percy's, which was fastened by a secret spring [concealed] in a particular part, which she described to me; and that most probably, from the difficulty of discovering this spring, Lord Ellrington yet retained the box unopened.

'Half-maddened by the idea of being that man's child whom of all others I most dreaded and detested, I went, scarcely knowing what I did, to Ellrington House. There, by entreaties, I prevailed on his lordship to show me the casket. I opened it, found the fatal document, glanced over its contents, and in a moment of anguish, consumed it in the flame of a candle which stood on the table.

'Now, my lord,' she continued, 'you know all my secret, and may, if you can, fathom the depth and weigh the burden of that misery under which my reason at times seems to totter. I hate explanation, and therefore shall condense what I have further to say into as brief a space as possible.'

When Marian had finished, the marquis asked her to describe to him the token by which she had recognized Henry Percy.

'It was', replied she, 'a small gold ring with a crystal stone containing a little of my hair braided, and my name written on the inside.'

'The vile old witch!' exclaimed Arthur. 'She bought it in Lapis's shop, and that fellow whom you saw is no more the person you took him to be than I am. As for the talk about Lord Ellrington, I doubt not it is a scandalous lie, and so I'll make her confess before the day is at an end.'

He then rang the bell and ordered three or four of the servants to go immediately to Harley Street and take Miss Foxley and whomever they might find with her into custody. They soon returned, accompanied by the governess and her male accomplice, whom my father and brother instantly recognized as Edward Percy, the well-known scamp and oldest brother to the youth whose character he had assumed. He unblushingly declared that his only motive for joining in the fraud was to extort a sum of money; and Miss Foxley, finding herself thus deserted by her assistant, confessed the falsity of all she had pretended and explained the mystery of the paper in the casket by saying, that such an agreement had really existed between the Ladies Hume and Percy, but had never been put in practice on account of their husbands' refusing to consent.

My father then told her that if she wished to escape punishment for her wickedness, she must instantly leave Africa for some distant country and never set foot on its shores again. 'I give you your choice', said the duke, 'between two evils—exile or the pillory. Choose that which you consider the least.'

She chose the former, and was accordingly shipped off the next day. As for Edward Percy, my father gave him ten sovereigns for his candid confession and dismissed him well satisfied.

'Do you forgive my involuntary disobedience now, Arthur?' asked the once more happy Marian, when all was settled.

A smile and a kiss answered her more satisfactorily than words. And thus ends my Tale of the Secret.

It was on the evening of the memorable sixteenth of March, the day of the great insurrection, that Mrs. Hart, a respectable widow-lady, and her daughter Lily sat by the parlour fireside of their quiet and modest mansion, situated in one of the remote suburbs of Verdopolis. They had passed the day in a state of the most intense and feverish anxiety, hourly expecting that the flames of war, which were raging with such violence in other parts of the city, would spread to the obscure quarter in which they dwelt. Happily, however, about three o'clock P.M. the incessant thunder of distant artillery, which till then they had heard pealing from the far-off eastern division, began to die away. The cloud of smoke which hung so gloomily between earth and heaven waxed less dense, the tumultuous roar of battle grew fainter, and intelligence soon arrived that the rebellion had at length been completely put down by Government.

Hours elapsed before the two terrified females could free themselves from the flutter of excitement in which they had been kept all day. But when night fell down and all continued quiet, when several fresh messengers confirmed the good news, and when many of those who had been engaged in the combat, returning to their homes, declared that the army of rebels was utterly cut off, they began to feel themselves reassured, and after bolting the doors and fastening the windows of the house, ventured for the first time since morning to partake of a slight meal, which Bessie, their only servant, had managed, though half dead with fear, to prepare. When it was concluded both drew near to the fire. As yet, they felt too unsettled to engage in their usual occupations of reading or sewing, but sat talking over the fearful events of the day and conjecturing the probable consequences of this unsuccessful attempt against good government. While they were thus employed, Lily suddenly stopped short in the midst of a sentence she was uttering:

'Listen, Mama', said she. 'Do you not hear a noise in the garden?'

Her mother listened. 'I do', she replied. 'It sounds like the moan of someone in pain; perhaps it may proceed from some poor wounded creature, and if so, it is our duty to assist him.'

With these words, she stepped to a little glass door which opened into the garden. Lily followed her mother. It was a clear and still night; the moon and stars were shining most brilliantly in a perfectly unclouded heaven, and their descending beams revealed the form of a human being stretched on the grass near a little wicket which was open. Mrs. Hart called to the prostrate figure, but received no answer. She then went up to him and took his hand. It was very cold; he had ceased moaning and now lay motionless.

'I fear he is dead', said the benevolent lady, in a tone of compassion, 'but hasten, Lily, and tell Bessie to run instantly for the nearest surgeon.'

'I know something of the art of surgery', said a voice close at hand, while a tall figure entered by the open wicket. 'And if my skill would be of any use, it is at your service, madam.'

'Who are you, sir?' asked she, in some alarm at this sudden intrusion.

'An officer in the Grand Army of Verdopolis, madam, and one whom no individual of the fair sex needs to fear.'

Encouraged by the soft and gentle accent in which the stranger spoke, she expressed her gratitude for his timely offer of assistance; and soon the wounded man was, with the additional aid of Bessie, conveyed into the snug little parlour and safely deposited on a sofa. As the candle-light fell on his pallid features, the officer uttered an exclamation of surpise.

'I know this person', said he; 'he is my dearest friend. I trust to God he yet lives. If not, Africa has this day sustained a great loss.'

He then hastened to revive him by means of stimulants and cordial waters, which Mrs. Hart liberally supplied. Gradually he returned to life, and on opening his eyes, stared wildly round and would have spoken, but his military medical attendant strictly forbade him to utter a word. On examination, his wound was found to consist in a bayonet stab in the right side; it was not deep, and most fortunately the vital parts remained uninjured.

'By what name shall I call your friend, sir?' asked Mrs. Hart, when the wound was staunched and bandaged and the poor sufferer put to bed.

'Mr. Seymour', replied the officer, after a moment's consideration. 'And my name is Colonel Percival. If I could venture to urge so bold a request, madam, I should wish him to remain here till he is completely cured. I will be your guarantee for the reimbursement of such expenses as you may incur on his account.'

Mrs. Hart assured him of her perfect willingness to permit the stranger's sojourn; and then, after promising to call again next morning, Colonel Percival took his leave.

'What a handsome man that officer is', said Lily Hart when he was gone. 'I never saw such dark and sparkling eyes or such a magnificent form and face. But he looks very young to be a colonel.'

'He does, my dear', replied her mother. 'Most probably, however, he is a scion of some noble family. At least, I should conjecture so from his lofty and patrician appearance; and they, you know, obtain preferment early.'

Days and weeks passed away, and Mr. Seymour recovered rapidly under the treatment of his friend, who attended him with the most assiduous and constant care. The invalid's manners at first were not very prepossessing, in the opinion of his kind hostesses. He appeared cold and distant, and seemed to take all the attentions bestowed upon him as his right; but upon longer acquaintance, this chilly reserve thawed almost entirely away. As his wound healed, he became more agreeable; and when, at length, he was able to leave his bedroom and sit in the armchair by the little parlour-hearth, Lily wondered how she could ever have thought him either a plain or a proud man.

In person he was very tall, and so erect as to appear at times rather stiff and formal. His features were regularly formed, his forehead lofty and open, his eyes of a dark grey colour, deep-set and piercing. A general air of dignified gravity pervaded his whole countenance and, notwithstanding his youth, for he did not appear to be above twenty-five or six years of age, became him extremely well. He never laughed, but the contrast of his usual sobriety imparted an uncommon graciousness to his smile; but notwithstanding all this, his disposition was evidently turned to a fondness for domestic life and female society. He would sit in a rustic seat in the garden, when he was able, weaving a garland of roses for the head of Lily or the neck of her favourite lap-dog. He constructed a pretty moss house and adorned it with shells and pebbles. At times, though not often, he would accompany Miss Hart's guitar with his powerful yet melodious voice; and regularly every morning, he gave her lessons in the Italian language, in which he appeared to be a proficient and which she was studying. Then in the evenings, when the curtains were let down and the fire burned bright, while the ladies sat at their needlework, Mr. Seymour would read to them from some standard author, commenting on remarkable passages as he went on and illustrating such as were obscure, in language so lucid, so unassuming, and at times so eloquent, as to give them a most exalted idea of his understanding. When he became earnest in conversation, which he often did if the subject interested him, his countenance grew very animated, his eyes sparkled, and his words flowed forth with freedom, energy, and even brilliancy.

Often when he was thus awakened, Lily would drop her work and gaze on him earnestly; and then, when the tide of inspired feeling gradually ebbed, and he returned to his customary calm and stately demeanour, she would reassume it with an involuntary sigh. Mrs. Hart marked this and many other little indications of her daughter's [growing] regard for their guest. When Mr. Seymour spoke, Lily was all rapt and earnest attention; when he was unusually grave, a sympathizing sadness appeared on her face. If the slightest complaint of returning pain or weakness escaped him, she trembled lest he should relapse; and if a lighter tread or a gayer strain of conversation proclaimed improving health and spirits, her joy knew no bounds. All these tokens of incipient affection were noticed by the careful mother and occasioned her many an hour of anxious meditation; for though she could easily discern the state of her daughter's mind, yet that of the stranger defied her penetration. He was so sedate, so guarded, possessed such complete command over himself, that it was utterly impossible to read his thoughts in his countenance.

True, Lily was handsome enough to attract the attention of any man; and so my readers would have thought had they seen her. She was about eighteen years old, rather above than under the middle size, elegantly formed, with gracefully rounded limbs and small fairylike face and hands. Her complexion was of a rich and sunny tone of colouring. Dark, bright eyes, softened by long, silken lashes, diffused a most fascinating expression over her sweet face, and harmonized well with the wild black curls which waved in such luxuriant clusters over her glowing vermilion cheeks. To these attractions were added a charming simplicity of dress and manner, all the refined accomplishments of a polite education, and the more solid advantages of a useful one. Yet this lovely creature failed to excite any emotion in the, in this respect, almost stoical Mr. Seymour, beyond what was indicated by an occasional fixed gaze, which was instantly withdrawn and compensated for by an additional degree of gravity and restraint.

In the space of two months he was, by dint of good nursing, restored to perfect health; but yet he did not seem willing to depart. One morning, while they were sitting at breakfast, Colonel Percival happened to call. After a little desultory conversation, he began to urge on his friend the necessity of returning to his family, who, he said, were beginning to be very anxious about him. Mr. Seymour made no answer to his arguments, but appeared very loath to acknowledge their justice.

At length, the colonel said laughingly, 'Well, if you still refuse to quit your quarters, I shall begin to think someone has cast a spell round you. Perhaps my fair Lily here could furnish me with the name of the enchantress, if she would.'

A deep blush crimsoned the young philosopher's brow; he started up directly and exclaimed, 'I will go this instant, I will quit this peaceful retreat without delay. Mrs. Hart, allow me to offer you a very slight compensation for your unwearied kindness and attention towards me.'

So saying, he tendered her a banknote of two hundred pounds. This, however, his disinterested hostess most promptly refused. In vain he implored her to accept it: she would not, and in the end he was compelled to return it to his pocket-book. Then, turning to Lily, he took her hand, pressed it gently, slipped off a valuable diamond ring which decorated his little finger, placed it on hers, and with a faint, mournful farewell, abruptly left the house. Colonel Percival looked after him a moment with a significant smile, bowed gracefully to both the ladies and wished them a good morning, and departed.

A year elapsed, and during that little space of time poor Lily saw many and mighty changes. She had wept the loss of a loved and loving mother, whom a grave illness had in seven days' time carried to her grave; she had been left destitute by the failure of a banker in whose hands the whole of her small though competent fortune was lodged; and she had been forced to leave the house where she was born and brought up, and now resided in an humble dwelling containing only two apartments, where she endeavoured to support herself by manufacturing and selling ornamental articles such as screens, racks, [etc.]. All day long she sat engaged in the production of the most beautiful and elegant forms, yet her utmost diligence could only procure her the means of a very scanty subsistence. In the meantime, [several words illegible] with grief for her dear parent's death and another deep-seated and hopeless sorrow greatly impaired her health. She grew thin and pale; her step lost its elasticity, her eye its lustre, her cheek its bloom; and in short she faded to the mere shadow of her former self.

Once evening, after toiling ten weary hours over scraps of cardboard and shreds of gilt paper, sick at heart with her thankless labour, she rose, and wrapping herself in a large mantle, left her house to seek relaxation in a short walk. Grateful was the freshness of the soft balmy summer's evening wind as it kissed her wasted cheek and played among her black, unbraided ringlets. The golden glory of a fast-westering sun lay on the distant harbour, brightened its busy shores, and lit up with a warm glow the rocklike structure which soars from the centre of magnificent Verdopolis. Unconscious whither her way tended, she paced slowly on, gazing now at the dazzling west, now at the far-off hills which shone dimly visible in the excess of radiance which suffused them, and now at the dark blue waters of the seemingly waveless sea. Such an assemblage of lovely objects quickly calmed her griefs and excited in her mind a train of soothing meditations. Ere long she was roused from her delicious reverie by a hum of human voices and a tread of passing footsteps, which warned her that she had left her own quiet quarter of the city and was entering upon a busier [illegible]. She looked up and saw that she was in the wide and splendid street called Ebor Terrace. Heaven-aspiring palaces of the most superb and imposing architecture rose on each side, and seemed in their princely pride to frown away any poor plebian who might chance to fix his eye on them. This street, as my readers well know, is the Grand Corso of Verdopolis; and now, at the fashionable hour of sunset, it was crowded with hundreds of equestrians and pedestrians. Here groups of patrician beauties, lustrous in the fascination of bright eyes, lovely lips, beaming gems, and nodding plumes, glided stately by; and as they went, a soft perfume, and a sweet murmur of silver tones, lingered on the breeze behind them. There a stately chariot with six or eight fiery horses passed full speed like a rushing whirlwind, and everywhere the noble and the beautiful moved like beings of another sphere, seeming to disdain the ground on which they trod. As poor Lily looked round on the glittering forms of life and splendour, not one of whom would condescend to cast a look or waste a thought on her, she felt a sensation of utter loneliness, and breathing a deep sigh, turned to depart.

While she was hastily retracing her steps, she chanced to glance upwards at one of the majestic edifices frowning above her and saw, seated at an open window and gazing pensively at the brilliant crowds beneath, the well-remembered form of Mr. Seymour. At this unexpected sight, a smothered exclamation of joyful surprise burst from Lily's lips and a radiant light sparkled in her dark eye. She stood transfixed for a moment; and while yet lost in wonder and delight, he raised his eyes and they fell on her. Blushing deeply, she hung down her head and covered her face with her hands; when she looked again the window was closed and the welcome vision departed.

'Cruel man', thought she, while a shower of unbidden tears gushed forth. 'He might have spoken one little word to me, were it only for the sake of my mother's kindness.'

The recollection of her mother determined Lily to visit the grave where her beloved ashes reposed, and with the tardy tread of sorrow she took the way to St. Michael's Cemetery. Twilight had quenched the glory of the setting sun in soft and silent shades ere she reached that huge wilderness of tombs, and a pale crescent moon was gilding the gloomy groves of gigantic cypress trees as she sat down near an upright headstone of grey marble, which stood close under the lofty southern wall. Utterly unbroken was the frozen hush which hung over that [city] of the dead. No step, no voice waked an echo among the silent tombs; but soon the cathedral clock tolled the hour of vespers, and then there came floating on the night air the swell of a solemn organ from the holy minster, which stood bathed in heavy moonbeams not far distant, and the sublime sound of a sacred song. As the chant died away, Lily took up the tune and sang mournfully the following stanzas:

> Dark is the mansion of the dead,
>   Dark, desolate, and still:
> Around it dwells a solemn dread,
>   Within a charnel chill.
>
> O Mother! does thy spirit rest
>   In fairer worlds than ours?
> 'Mid tranquil valleys ever-blest,
>   And ever-blooming bowers?
>
> I trust it doth, for thy pale clay
>   Hath found no fair abode,
> Shut from the happy light of day,
>   Pressed by the cold earth's load.
>
> Yet Mother! I would rest with thee
>   In thy long dreamless sleep.
> Though dread its mute solemnity,
>   All voiceless, still and deep.
>
> And I would rest my weary head
>   Upon thy lifeless breast,
> Nor feel one shuddering thrill of dread
>   At what my temples prest.
>
> Earth is a dreary void to me,
>   Heaven is a cloud of gloom.
> Then Mother! let me sleep with thee,
>   Safe in thy stilly tomb.

She ceased, and throwing herself on the grassy grave, wept and sobbed bitterly. When this paroxysm of grief subsided, she rose, and was preparing to leave the cemetery, when a tall and dark figure glided from an adjoining cypress grove and stood before her. Overcome with terror at this unexpected apparition, she shrieked aloud.

'Does Miss Hart fear him whose life she saved?' said a deep calm voice. Lily answered not, but seized with sudden faintness, sank on a stone which stood near. The stranger seated himself beside her and took her passive hand. 'Has my Lily forgotten the ungrateful Seymour?' he asked in soothing accents.

'No! Never! Never!' was her enthusiastic reply. 'Nor will I, till death separates me from all mental associations.'

'From what I have just heard', said he, 'you have lost your earthly protector and are now left desolate in the world.'

'I am', replied she briefly.

He paused a moment and then said, 'Lily, you have doubtless by this time concluded that I have lost all recollection of you and your [household], but it is not so. I have striven indeed to forget you, laboured night and day to erase the impress of your too-dear image from my mind. To this end, I have sought the drawing-room and the ballroom, in order to find some form of superior loveliness, some mind of higher excellence, than those which haunted me like a heavenly vision. But in vain: not one could I discover amongst all the fairest and noblest of the land to vie with my peerless, my lovely Lily. At length, unable any longer to live without you, I determined, despite of foolish prejudice and family pride, to seek out the poor widow's daughter and gain her consent to a private union. With this resolution, I went about six months since to your house in the eastern suburbs, but it was empty and none knew whither you were gone. Since that time I have sought you, but in vain, till this evening, when I was gazing at the [groups] in Ebor Terrace, my eye rested on the long-desired form. I immediately quitted the house where I was, watched what way you took, followed you hither. And now, Miss Hart, will you be my wife or not? Say yes and you make a fellow creature happy for life; say no and you pronounce the death-doom of one who never wronged you.'

After such an appeal, who could have uttered the cold and chilling negation? Lily could not: she saw at her feet the grave, the philosophical Mr. Seymour, he who seemed to have subdued all the turbulent passions which agitate other men; she beheld him changed for her sake into a mere mortal lover; she heard him declare that his life's happiness depended on her decision; and she murmured a faint and faltering 'yes!'

'Bless you, my dearest!' exclaimed he with energy, while he snatched her hand and pressed it passionately to his lips. 'Bless you for that little word! You are now mine and mine alone, and nothing save death shall divide us.' After a pause, he continued in his usual composed and deliberate manner. 'Circumstances, Miss Hart, which I cannot now explain to you render it imperative that our union should be strictly private. Do you agree to this?'

'I do', she replied, for having unconditionally yielded the grand point, she could not now hesitate about trifles.

'Meet me, then', proceeded Mr. Seymour, 'tomorrow night at this hour in this place.'

She consented, and after one long and fervent embrace they parted. Some of my readers will doubtless consider that this was an imprudent transaction on the part of Lily, but let them remember that she loved Mr. Seymour more than her life, that besides him there was not one creature on earth in whom she could centre her stock of warm affections, and that she was a young and inexperienced girl who had not yet completed her nineteenth year.

The whole of the next day Lily employed in making her bridal attire, and when it began to grow dark she dressed herself in it. It was a gown of a dark-coloured silk such as suited well with her complexion, ornamented here and there with small knots of pink ribbon. A larger bow of the same material bound up the rich jetty tresses which otherwise would have hung lower than her waist and made them form a natural coronet on the top of her head. Thus simply arrayed she looked most lovely; excitement had restored the bright rose to her cheek and the lustrous light to her eye. And when wrapped in her dark mantle she again passed over Ebor Terrace, there was none amongst all the hundreds there whose tread was so bounding and elastic as her own.

The crescent moon was again rising when she entered St. Michael's Cemetery. A gusty, hollow-toned wind waved the great arms of the cypress trees as they stood like swart giants rising darkly against the twilight sky, and the last swell of the vesper organ was dying in the domed cathedral. Solemn and mournful were the sights and sounds of that darkling hour, but her buoyant spirits resisted the gloomy impression they were calculated to make, and full of happy anticipation she sought her mother's tomb. Her heart bounded as she saw a tall figure standing beside it, but on drawing nearer she perceived that it was not her lover but a military officer dressed in uniform; his sword and steel-clasped belt sparkled in the moonlight, and as he paced slowly to and fro with measured step he hummed the fragment of a merry march. Filled with dismay, she was about to retreat, when he suddenly raised his head and exclaimed, 'Is that you, Miss Hart?'

In the pronunciation of these words, Lily instantly recognized the deep melody of Colonel Percival's peculiarly fascinating voice, and the stranger's face being now turned to the light, she likewise knew the statuelike and noble beauty of his features. Now Lily had always admired the colonel because he was a handsome and graceful man, but she feared him likewise on account of a certain lofty imperiousness in his manner and in the expression of his bright and bold, dark eyes. His behaviour to her mother and herself had ever been perfectly kind and gentle, but there was a certain air of condescension mixed with it which, whenever she conversed with him, used to impress her with an indescribable feeling of awe. It was, therefore, with considerable misgiving and in a very timid tone that she answered his question in the affirmative.

'Do not be afraid, fair Lily', said he encouragingly. 'I am here on behalf of my friend, Mr. Seymour, who was prevented from coming himself to meet you by urgent business, any neglect of which would have excited inquiry and perhaps discovery, in which case the happiness he has so much at heart would infallibly have been snatched away from him at the moment of its completion. I hope you will not refuse to allow me to act as his substitute.'

Lily had gone too far to retreat, and she was therefore reluctantly compelled to accept the gay young officer as a conductor. When she had signified that she was ready to follow him, he uttered a shrill whistle, and immediately a splendid carriage dashed through the open gates of the cemetery. Having assisted her to enter it and placed himself by her side, he gave the word of departure, and off they rolled with the [celerity] of lightning.

The carriage blinds being down, Lily could not discern which way they went, but after an hour's rapid driving the vehicle suddenly drew up and Colonel Percival informed her that she must now alight. On getting out she saw before her the pillared entrance of a vast park. A footman unfolded the gates, and her guide, drawing her arm through his, proceeded to follow the carriage road till they came in sight of a most extensive and magnificent mansion, or rather palace, whose white marble columns and turrets were all gleaming with softest radiance in the tranquil moonbeams. He then turned, crossed an angle of the park and, opening a small arched door which was formed in a lofty wall by which this portion of the grounds was bounded, they entered a large garden. After threading their way through long [illegible] dark alleys through whose bowery arches scarcely a ray of light found ingress, and crossing open parterres where the closed and drooping blossoms and variegated green leaves were all wet and glittering with the tears of night, they at length reached a small chapel or oratory situated in the midst of a great wilderness of tall and fragrant flowering shrubs.

'Now,' whispered the colonel as they passed under the fretted porch and up the long echoing aisle, 'Now, fair Lily, I have discharged my trust and shall yield you to better hands.'

'And you have discharged it well', said the voice of Mr. Seymour, issuing from a neighbouring aisle. 'Adrian, I thank you, but do not depart till you have seen the indissoluble knot tied.'

He consented to remain in order to witness their union, and all three proceeded towards the altar, where a clergyman of a remarkably grave and venerable aspect stood ready in gown and cassock. In another quarter of an hour Lily Hart had changed her name and pledged her faith for life.

When the marriage ceremony was over, Percival took his friend's hand, warmly wished him joy, bade him farewell, and, after respectfully saluting the bride, departed.

'Now, my own dear Lily,' said Mr. Seymour, turning to his wife, 'we must leave Verdopolis without delay, if you do not already feel too much fatigued.'

Lily assured him that she was not at all tired, and leaving the chapel they returned to the park gate, where the carriage still awaited their arrival.

All night long their journey continued, and at last, just about sunrise, Mr. Seymour lifted one of the carriage blinds and bade his wife look out. She did so, and her eye beheld one of the fairest and most fertile scenes imagination can conceive. Emerald-green meadows stretched on every side, spotted here and there with tall, spreading forest trees and watered by a broad and placid river on whose banks, facing the east and bathed in the rosy light of early day, there appeared a small and elegant villa surrounded by a lawn and gardens and backed by a grove of tall young elm trees, whose branches, as they were shaken by the sweet morning wind, let fall a shower of dew on the clustering vines and roses which clung to its roof and sides.

'What a lovely place', said Lily. 'I should like to live there.'

'Your wish is granted, my love,' replied her husband, 'for that is your destined place of abode.'

And for three years Lily dwelt in this peaceful little paradise, in the midst of as perfect happiness as it is possible for mortal man or woman to enjoy. Surrounded by all the elegancies and comforts of life, blessed ere long by a beautiful and healthy boy, cherished by an affectionate and tender husband whose mild philosophical manners and calm, deep attachment never lost either their charm or their strength, who could be happy if she was not?

Yet there were one or two little circumstances which somewhat disturbed her felicity. In the first place, the mystery of their clandestine marriage still remained unsolved. She did not yet properly know who her husband was; she had never seen one member of his family or even heard him mention them. His anxiety to keep her in perfect seclusion was evident; he never once permitted her to visit Verdopolis, and no guest with the exception of Colonel Percival was ever allowed to enter Elm Grove Villa. In the second place, she was often for weeks together deprived of Mr. Seymour's own society. He seldom upon an aggregate spent more than the fourth part of the year with her, the rest being devoted to important business in the city. It is true, the brevity and fewness of his visits rendered them more delightful, but notwithstanding this, she could not help occasionally expressing a wish that she might see more of one so justly dear to her.

One evening at the commencement of the fourth year of her marriage, she, her husband, and Colonel Percival (whom Lily had learned [to] regard not only without fear but with feelings of the warmest and purest friendship) were all assembled in the villa drawing-room. It was a wild and tempestuous night. Torrents of rain dashed incessantly against the windows; a gusty wind swept in fierce but wailing howls through the crashing elm grove; and every now and then its melancholy voice was mingled with the dull muttering of distant thunder. This war of elements without the villa, however, seemed only to increase the cheerfulness of the party within. Lily, seated at her harp, was uttering tones melodious enough, one would have thought, to have charmed the wildest storm that ever rushed with blast and thunder through the midnight heavens. Her husband bent over her, listening in rapt attention to the sweetness of her voice and harp. As for Colonel Percival, he was busily engaged with his pet, little Augustus Seymour, now tossing him in his arms, now dancing before his dazzled eyes a glittering watch and chain, and then again teaching him how to handle and cock a small pistol which he loaded with powder and discharged once or twice, at which the bold, spirited child, instead of being terrified, clapped his hands and chuckled with delight at every explosion.

'Colonel,' said Lily, rising when she had ceased her song and advancing towards him with a smile, 'you will spoil my child by your too-great indulgence. Already he is getting as willful and unmanageable as— as—'

'As myself, madam, you would say', interrupted the colonel, laughing. 'Be it so, I have no desire to see him otherwise. If he could unite a little of my impetuosity with his father's wisdom, he would be perfect, you know.'

She was going to reply in the same half-playful, half-serious strain, when a tremendous peal of thunder burst just over their heads.

'The storm increases', observed Mr. Seymour. 'How dreadful must be the situation of those who are exposed to its fury.'

He had scarcely uttered these words when the sound of approaching carriage wheels, followed by a violent ringing of the door-bell and a correspondingly vigorous agitation of the knocker, proclaimed that there were persons without who suffered even now the pitiless drenching of the tempest. Directly after, a servant opened the door and announced that a gentleman and two ladies had arrived in an open chariot and requested shelter till the storm should pass over.

'Show them into the dining-room', said Mr. Seymour.

'The fire is gone out in that room, sir', replied the servant, 'and they are dripping wet.'

'Well, then, bring them here. I suppose, Adrian (looking toward the colonel), they are not persons who know anything of us, so it does not much signify.'

Steps were now heard on the staircase, the door was again flung open, and there entered first a tall, perpendicular, rigid-looking old gentleman of about sixty, with high bald forehead trimmed with a fringe of silver hair, aquiline nose, and very keen, piercing grey eyes. Then a lady who had passed the meridian of life but still retained in her benevolent countenance and mild blue eyes the remains of what had once been surpassing loveliness, and lastly a tall, slender, and beautiful girl. Both the ladies were enveloped in large dark velvet mantles lined with costly ermine; these rich garments were wet through and clung round them as if they had been flimsy taffeta.

The effect which the appearance of this imposing trio produced upon Percival and Seymour seemed very unaccountable to Lily. The former sprang up, exclaiming with an astonished smile, 'Lord bless me, the day of discovery is come at last, the hour when the secrets of all hearts shall be revealed. But never mind, John, stand it out boldly like a man. Flinch not, lie not, but make a clean bosom and take what shall come thereafter.'

Mr. Seymour did not seem greatly to need this advice. He had stood up and with folded arms and an air of cool determination had taken his station just opposite the door.

'What means all this, my lord Marquis?' asked the old gentleman, looking sternly at Colonel Percival. 'Why do I find you and my son here, and who is this woman?'

'That woman,' replied Seymour in a firm but respectful tone, 'that woman, my royal father, is my dear wife Lily, Marchioness of Fidena. I crowned her with my coronet three years since, and there by her side stands my son and your grandson, John Augustus Sneaky.'

The appearance of a thousand disembodied spirits could not have striken the royal party with more mute astonishment than did this simple piece of intelligence. At length, after gazing at his son silently for some minutes, the monarch Alexander spoke:

'Do not think to impose on me thus', he said. 'That presumptuous woman shall return immediately to her native obscurity, from which you have so wickedly raised her, unless you can produce the fullest proof of your marriage and unless that marriage was solemnized by the Chief Prelate, for no humbler priest can lawfully wed a prince of the blood.'

'I can bear witness to your majesty', replied Colonel Percival, or as we must now call him, the Marquis of Douro, for such he really was, 'that about this time three years since, John, Prince of Fidena, was united to Lily Hart by Gravey, the Metropolitan Archbishop himself, before the high altar of the private chapel situated in the gardens which surround your imperial palace on the banks of the Niger, I standing by and giving away the bride with my own hands.'

A dark and ominous flush covered Alexander's haughty brow when he heard this pronounced by the unabashed marquis in a tone of the most perfect and easy nonchalance. What he would have said or done I know not, but just as he was about to speak, the queen and her eldest daughter Lady Edith (my readers will have already recognized these exalted personages in the two females who accompanied him) flung themselves at his feet and implored him to forgive what could not now be undone and to receive once more to his paternal favour the son who till now had never offended him. Lily, trembling like an aspen leaf and pale as her floral namesake, joined her tears to their entreaties. Alexander, however, remained quite unmoved by their supplications and would probably have given free vent to the indignation which boiled within him, had not the Marquis of Douro stepped up to him and whispered in a low, emphatic tone:

'Monarch of the mountains, you may indeed cast this son away, but where will you turn to find another? Who shall be more worthy to inherit your crown and throne? Nowhere: therefore royalty must depart from your line and the sceptre pass into the hands of aliens.'

'You have spoken truth', replied the twelve* after a pause. 'Therefore, Prince John, I forgive you: but take notice it is not from the weakness of compassion, but merely because necessity compels me to it. Had I another son who was yet guiltless of any such daring act of disobedience, I would disown you, your wife, and child instantly and forever.'

Prince John made no answer to this speech of his royal father's; he only bowed low, and raising his kneeling wife said, with a pride almost equal to that of Alexander himself, 'Now, my Lily, you shall appear in the circles for which nature designed you, and if anyone dare breathe a word of scorn against you or yours, by heaven, that word shall be his last.'

On Monday last, the Marchioness of Fidena made her first public appearance in Verdopolis at a grand ball given on the occasion at Elimbos Palace, the residence of the king her father-in-law. I saw her and can safely state that Lily Hart, the widow's daughter, is worthy for grace and beauty to rank with the noblest born and fairest of Verdopolis.

---

* As used here, twelve is a title, roughly equivalent to a title such as 'apostle'. Alexander Sneaky was one of the original twelve toy soldiers, thus one of the founders of the Glasstown Confederacy. They were sometimes referred to collectively as The Twelves, hence the singular term used here.

Afterword

Children   The Brontë sisters—Charlotte, Emily, and Anne—form
of Genius   a grouping unique in our literature: certainly no other
three sisters have approached their combined accom-
plishments as novelists. Charlotte's *Jane Eyre* and Emily's *Wuthering
Heights* have become standard texts in our schools and colleges, and the
readers whose interests are kindled by these works may find their way to
Charlotte's *Villette*—better, some will say, than *Jane Eyre*—or to her less
satisfying *Shirley* or *The Professor*. They may look in vain for another novel
by Emily, but they may also discover the quiet power of Anne's *Agnes
Grey* or the sprawling horror of *The Tenant of Wildfell Hall*. Some will argue
whether Charlotte or Emily is the greater talent, while most will agree that
Anne is third in this company but never third-rate. It is a remarkable con-
centration of genius, and its origins lie in a childhood history as remarkable
as any story the sisters wrote. Out of this childhood history come the two
recently discovered tales by Charlotte that are offered in this volume.

In this earlier period, before the sisters' fame, two other figures rise up to
meet us: a father whose influence on his children was immense and a
brother whose influence on his sisters was probably greater than theirs
upon each other. The Reverend Patrick Brontë was a man of substantial
talent in his own right, who raised himself from humble rural Irish origins
to a Cambridge degree and ordination in the Church of England. His
marriage to Maria Branwell brought him six children; the two oldest,
Maria and Elizabeth, died at ages of eleven and ten, a few years after their
mother's untimely death. The remaining children—the three sisters and
brother Branwell—seem to have turned toward each other for emotional
support while observing in their father a model of intellectual activity.

The picture of home life that we glean from the records is fascinating:
a forcing bed for genius, it might be called, and certainly far from the norms
of the modern school and family. With none of the distractions of radio,
television, or telephone; with little of the lock-step routine of formal
classroom training; the Brontë children developed with an astounding
precocity. They read widely in the English classics and in contemporary
poetry; they read the weekly press and the monthly magazines that came

into their home; and they discussed literature, politics, and current events among themselves and with their father, who treated them as his intellectual equals. Patrick Brontë, himself the author of several religious books, not only exemplified the importance of writing but also the strenuous exercise of the moral imagination. The following anecdote, recalled by Patrick in his old age, suggests something of the Brontë children's life with their father.

'I frequently thought that I discovered signs of rising talent, which I had seldom or never before seen in any of their age. . . . A circumstance now occurs to my mind which I may as well mention. When my children were very young, when, as far as I can remember, the oldest was about ten years of age, and the youngest about four, thinking that they knew more than I had yet discovered, in order to make them speak with less timidity, I deemed that if they were put under a sort of cover I might gain my end; and happening to have a mask in the house, I told them all to stand back and speak boldly from under cover of the mask.

'I began with the youngest (Anne, afterwards Acton Bell), and asked what a child like her most wanted; she answered, "Age and experience." I asked the next (Emily, afterwards Ellis Bell) what I had best do with her brother, Branwell, who was sometimes a naughty boy; she answered, "Reason with him, and when he won't listen to reason whip him." I asked Branwell what was the best way of knowing the difference between the intellects of man and woman; he answered, "By considering the difference between them as to their bodies." I then asked Charlotte what was the best book in the world; she answered, "The Bible." And what was the next best; she answered, "The Book of Nature." I then asked the next what was the best mode of education for a woman; she answered, "That which would make her rule her house well." Lastly, I asked the oldest what was the best mode of spending time; she answered, "By laying it out in preparation for a happy eternity." I may not have given precisely their words, but I have nearly done so, as they made a deep and lasting impression on my memory. The substance, however, was exactly what I have stated.'

But the children had a private life as well, in which another kind of imagination—we now call it mythic—worked upon their reading and their limited experience with the world. One of Charlotte's earliest manuscripts hints at its nature:

'June the 31st, 1829.

'The play of the "Islanders" was formed in December 1827, in the following manner: One night, about the time when the cold sleet and stormy fogs of November are succeeded by the snowstorms, and high, piercing night winds of confirmed winter, we were all sitting round the warm blazing kitchen fire, having just concluded a quarrel with Tabby concerning the propriety of lighting a candle, from which she came off victorious, no candle having been produced. A long pause succeeded, which was at last broken by Branwell saying, in a lazy manner, "I don't know what to do." This was echoed by Emily and Anne.

'Tabby. "Wha, ya may go t' bed."
'Branwell. "I'd rather do anything than that."
'Charlotte. "Why are you so glum to-night, Tabby? Oh! suppose we had each an island of our own."
'Branwell. "If we had I would choose the Island of Man."
'Charlotte. "And I would choose the Isle of Wight."
'Emily. "The Isle of Arran for me."
'Anne. "And mine shall be Guernsey."

'We then chose who should be chief men in our islands. Branwell chose John Bull, Astley Cooper, and Leigh Hunt; Emily, Walter Scott, Mr. Lockhart, Johnny Lockhart; Anne, Michael Sadler, Lord Bentinck, Sir Henry Halford. I chose the Duke of Wellington and two sons, Christopher North and Co., and Mr. Abernethy. Here our conversation was interrupted by the, to us, dismal sound of the clock striking seven, and we were summoned off to bed. The next day we added many others to our list of men, till we got almost all the chief men of the kingdom. After this, for a long time, nothing worth noticing occurred. In June 1828 we erected a school on a fictitious island, which was to contain 1,000 children. The manner of the building was as follows: The Island was fifty miles in circumference, and certainly appeared more like the work of enchantment than anything real,' &c.

At about the same time she also noted that "all our plays are very strange ones. Their nature I need not write on paper, for I think I shall always remember them."[1]

---

1. These excerpts are from *The Life of Charlotte Brontë*, 2 vols. (London, 1857), by Charlotte's close friend Elizabeth Gaskell. See 1: 59, 86–89.

And so they grew—Charlotte, Branwell, Emily, and Anne—differently but quite naturally into a life of writing. Branwell's career was to be pathetically short, spanning only his juvenile years; but the spectacle of his moral failure and physical ruin was to penetrate the imaginative life of each of his sisters. And although our subject here is Charlotte's writing, Branwell figures importantly in the account.

Childhood "The Secret" and "Lily Hart" are part of one of the
Writings most fascinating childhood enterprises recorded in our
literature. It all began when Patrick Brontë brought home for Branwell a simple gift—a set of twelve wooden soldiers. The impact upon the receptive imaginations of the talented Brontë children was immediate and intense: each claimed and named one soldier as a special hero. The figures thus born into fictive existence were nourished in the rich imaginative atmosphere of the children's daily life and became the leading characters in a series of "plays," as Charlotte called them: interconnected stories of the Twelve Adventurers, their founding of a kingdom in Africa, and the subsequent exploits of their descendants and the followers that soon populated the various provinces of this imaginary land.

Our attention must focus on Charlotte and, to a lesser extent, on Branwell; for in time Emily and Anne withdrew from the original enterprise to develop a separate mythical kingdom. Charlotte and Branwell, however, continued to elaborate the narrative of The Twelves, as the heroes came to be called, in a series of miniature hand-printed books, presumably proportioned to the size of the original toy figures. Charlotte's chosen soldier had been named after the Duke of Wellington, reflecting her enthusiasm for England's national hero. He was soon established as the ruler of his own African kingdom; others of the heroes were assigned their kingdoms in a loose confederation centering in The Great Glass Town, later called Verdopolis. "The dark hinterland of the novels," an artistic and moral "chaos," Kathleen Tillotson has called these uniquely cooperative, involuted, and self-referential early tales by Charlotte and Branwell:

Since [the tales] themselves issued from a corporate daydream, nothing ever needed to be explained; each piece assumed a knowledge not only of all the rest but of much that was "made out" only in talk or solitary imaginings. As the amorphous mass swelled and sprawled, it became impossible to envisage "outside" readers; the large problems of structure, the delicate question of guiding the interest—in a word, of communication—were never faced. There is no Angrian story that can be read with the serene confidence that, whatever happens, the writer is in control.[2]

The control, artistic and moral, Charlotte would achieve; but only by way of outgrowing Branwell and the Angrian tales into a disciplined life of writing. At this early stage, however, her brother's mark lies heavily upon Charlotte's work: both of the stories here presented assume a background of his creation.

This background was largely a realm of military adventure and political intrigue. Charlotte's imagination, however, turned to the themes of passion and suffering, which she explored mainly through the career of a second-generation hero, Arthur Augustus Adrian Wellesley, Marquis of Douro and later Duke of Zamorna and Emperor of Angria. Douro, as she called him in the earlier tales, grew largely out of her adolescent reading of Byron: nobly handsome, fatally attractive to almost every woman, Douro united in one frame all the talents of poet, warrior, and statesman. From her thirteenth to her twenty-third years, Charlotte chronicled his many loves and political vicissitudes; eventually he re-emerges as the Rochester of *Jane Eyre*. Perhaps as a defense against uncritical indulgence, she chose to write of her hero from the point of view of his critical, envious younger brother, Lord Charles Wellesley. Lord Charles (whose name echoes Charlotte's) is the narrator of both tales here presented. Douro's personal life provides the subject of "The Secret," while "Lily Hart" involves peripheral figures caught up in the civil disorder at which Douro is the center.

These tales come approximately midway in Charlotte's elaboration of the Glass Town epic. In this larger context, it is the precocity and persistence of the impulse to write that is more impressive than any individual performance; and these two tales do betray the inevitable awkwardness of a juvenile writer, particularly in their huddled conclusions. Indeed, the whole Brontë juvenile canon raises very clearly the problem of the "value"

---

2. Kathleen Tillotson, *Novels of the Eighteen-Forties* (Oxford, 1954), pp. 270–71.

of the immature work of writers who achieve mature masterpieces. The appropriate question, of course, is that of genesis, not only of imaginative power but of theme and technique to embody that power. Little I might say in this regard would add to what Fannie Ratchford has bequeathed to Brontë scholars in her landmark study of the juvenilia.[3] For the more casual reader, however, who has perhaps felt the force of *Jane Eyre* and who may smile indulgently at these slight but charming tales, I would offer some hint of the creative energy seeking expression at this early stage.

The most curious evidence, perhaps, comes in one of the earliest of the tales, written when Charlotte was fourteen. Her narrator, Lord Charles, finds himself caught up mysteriously in an intersection of his world and the supervening order of his creator, as Charlotte dramatizes the power of the creative imagination:

> It seemed as if I was a non-existent shadow—that I neither spoke, eat [*sic*], imagined, or lived of myself, but I was the mere idea of some other creature's brain. The Glass Town seemed so likewise. My father, Arthur, and everyone with whom I am acquainted, passed into a state of annihilation. . . . at the end of a long vista, as it were, appeared dimly and indistinctly, beings that really lived in a tangible shape, that were called by our names and were US from whom WE had been copied by something—I could not tell what.
>
> . . . I was roused by a loud noise above my head. I looked up and thick obscurity was before my eyes. Voices—one like my own but larger and dimmer (if sound may be characterised by such epithets) and another, which sounded familiar, yet I had never that I could remember heard it before—murmuring unceasingly in my ears.
>
> I saw books removing from the top shelves and returning, apparently of their own accord. By degrees the mistiness cleared off. I felt myself raised suddenly to the ceiling, and ere I was aware, behold two immense sparkling bright blue globes within a few yards of me. I was in a hand wide enough almost to grasp the Tower of all Nations, and when it lowered me to the floor I saw a huge personification of myself—hundreds of feet high—standing against the great Oriel.
>
> This filled me with a weight of astonishment greater than the mind

3. Fannie Ratchford, *The Brontës' Web of Childhood* (New York, 1941). With every other student of Brontë juvenilia, I am fundamentally indebted to this work.

of man ever before had to endure, and I was now perfectly convinced of my non-existence except in another corporeal frame which dwelt in the real world, for ours I thought was nothing but idea.[4]

More direct testimony appears later, when Charlotte writes in her own person of the intensity of her commitment to the creatures of her imagination:

I hear them speak . . . I see distinctly their figures—and though alone, I experience all the feelings of one admitted for the first time into a grand circle of classic beings—recognising by tone, gesture and aspect hundreds whom I never saw before, but whom I have heard of many a time, and is not this enjoyment? . . . There is one just now crossing—a lady I will not write her name though I know it—no history is connected with her identity, she is not one of the transcendantly [sic] fair and inaccessible sacred beings—whose fates are interwoven with the highest of the high— I cannot write of them except in total solitude I scarce dare think of them.[5]

As we contemplate, then, the achieved power of *Jane Eyre* and *Villette*, we must recognize that they did not spring unprecedented from a mind turned late to fiction. Rather, they are the culmination of a passionate life of writing. The early efforts, such as the tales here presented, are diminutive and crudely drawn; but they tap the impulse of genius and cast long shadows forward toward her mature work. The way to that work was to be by arduous renunciation, as she reluctantly turned from indulgence in dream and fantasy to the discipline of the realistic novel. The transition took place gradually: as early as 1839, she rehearsed in a fragmentary passage the leave-taking that would be complete by 1846, the date of her first-written but last-published novel, *The Professor*. The earlier manuscript records the crucial change of mood with regret:

I have now written a great many books and for a long time have dwelt on the same characters and scenes and subjects. . . but we must change,

4. "Strange Events," *The Young Men's Magazine* (December 1830), in *The Miscellaneous and Unpublished Writings of Charlotte and Patrick Branwell Brontë*, ed. T. J. Wise and J. A. Symington (London, 1936–1938), 8:19–20.

5. "Roe Head Journal" (1836). Quoted from Winifred Gérin, *Charlotte Brontë: The Evolution of Genius* (Oxford, 1967), p. 106. This collection of fragmentary jottings shows clearly how Charlotte was literally possessed by the creatures of her imagination.

for the eye is tired of the picture so oft recurring and now so familiar.

Yet do not urge me too fast, reader: it is no easy theme to dismiss from my imagination the images which have filled it so long; they were my friends and my intimate acquaintances. . . . Still, I long to quit for awhile that burning clime where we have sojourned too long—its skies aflame— the glow of sunset is always upon it—the mind would cease from excitement and turn now to a cooler region where the dawn breaks grey and sober, and the coming day for a time at least is subdued by clouds.[6]

By the time of *The Professor*, the scrupulous damping of her fancy produced a work so austere that it would be published only after her death, when her renown would assure an audience that the novel alone could not have gained earlier. The preface, written in retrospect after she had attained fame, gives us some notion of the strictures she had placed on herself:

I had got over any such taste as I might once have had for ornamented and redundant composition, and come to prefer what was plain and homely. . . .

I said to myself that my hero should work his way through life as I had seen real living men work theirs—that he should never get a shilling he had not earned—that no sudden turns should lift him in a moment to wealth and high station; that whatever small competency he might gain, should be won by the sweat of his brow; that, before he could find so much as an arbour to sit down in, he should master at least half the ascent of "the Hill of Difficulty;" that he should not even marry a beautiful girl or a lady of rank. As Adam's son he should share Adam's doom, and drain throughout life a mixed and moderate cup of enjoyment.[7]

Such extreme restraint, however, was not her natural mode, as every reader of *Jane Eyre* will recognize; and even *Villette*, a reworking of much of the material of *The Professor*, is in fact an accommodation of this program to her earlier mode—clumsily, in the Gothic claptrap of the ghostly nun, artfully in the prolonged analysis of Lucy Snowe's emotional trauma. The two tales that follow will give a fair representation of the "burning clime" of her early years that would be naturalized and rationalized—but never wholly denied—in her mature fiction.

---

6. "The Last of Angria," Wise and Symington, 9:403-4.
7. Quoted here from the Shakespeare Head edition.

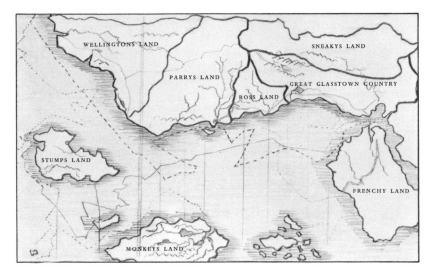

The Great Glasstown Confederacy, from a drawing by Branwell Brontë.

For Further Reading The reader interested in further exploration can begin with Fannie Ratchford's painstaking reconstruction of the saga in *The Brontës' Web of Childhood* (New York, 1941), based on her study of most of the surviving manuscripts. Many of these are transcribed in volumes 8–9 of the Shakespeare Head edition of the Brontës' *Works*, edited by T. J. Wise and J. A. Symington. Selected tales are printed in *Legends of Angria*, edited by Fannie Ratchford and William Clyde DeVane (New Haven, 1933); *The Twelve Adventurers and Other Stories*, edited by C. W. Hatfield (London, 1925); *Tales from Angria*, edited by Phillis Bentley (London, 1954); and *Five Novelettes*, edited by Winifred Gérin (London, 1971) Individual tales published separately include *The Spell: An Extravaganza*, edited by G. E. McLean (London, 1931); "A Leaf from an Unopened Volume," edited by A. Edward Newton in his *Derby Day and Other Adventures* (Boston, 1934); "An Interesting Passage," edited by Judith Chernaik, *London Times Literary Supplement* (23 November 1973); and "The Search After Hapiness [*sic*]," edited by T. A. J. Burnett (London and New York, 1969).

"The Secret"   The focus in "The Secret" falls not upon Charlotte's major hero, Douro, but upon his delicate child bride Marian Hume and his archrival Sir Alexander Percy. Marian is presented to us at approximately the midpoint of her brief marriage to Douro. Earlier Charlotte had recorded their idyllic courtship and betrothal; later Marian is supplanted in Douro's affections by the more assertively passionate Mary Percy, daughter of Alexander Percy by an earlier marriage than the one here described. In this tale, Percy's second marriage, to Zenobia Ellrington, has elevated him from a mere adventurer to the nobility; for Zenobia, it is a painful bondage, exacerbated by the fact that earlier she had been Marian's rival for Douro's love. But her sterner character serves her better than Marian's pliant nature: she survives, even as Douro's affections turn to her step-daughter, while the abandoned Marian dies of grief, attended by the noble John of Fidena.[8]

Percy we encounter here shortly after his metamorphosis in Charlotte's imagination from the pirate Alexander Rogue introduced into the tales by Branwell. Throughout the subsequent narratives he remains Douro's major antagonist: a brilliant, dissolute, unprincipled demagogue, at one point leading a civil insurrection and at another striking an uneasy alliance as premier in Douro's new kingdom of Angria.[9] The relationship is one of

---

8. This tangle of relationships emerges from "Albion and Marina" (1830), "The Bridal" (1832), "A Peep into a Picture Book" (1834), in *The Miscellaneous and Unpublished Writings of Charlotte and Patrick Branwell Brontë*, ed. T. J. Wise and J. A. Symington (London, 1936–1938), 8:24, 202, 358–60 (these tales by Charlotte); and from "The Pirate" (1833), Wise and Symington, 8:170 (by Branwell). See also Fannie Ratchford, *The Brontës' Web of Childhood* (New York, 1941), summary, pp. 73–76.

9. He is the revolutionary leader executed at the end of the civil war described in Branwell's "Letters from an Englishman," (1830–1832), Wise and Symington, 8:96. Resurrected, he is given an earlier history by Charlotte in "The Green Dwarf" (1833), conveniently readable in Fannie Ratchford and William Clyde DeVane, *Legends of Angria* (New Haven, 1933), pp. 1–102. As Douro's premier he ultimately engages in a conspiracy that sends Douro temporarily into exile. Upon Douro's regaining ascendancy, he and Percy reach an uneasy truce, the last complication being Douro's affair with Percy's nubile daughter, Caroline Vernon. Part of this series of events is Branwell's, part Charlotte's: for a convenient summary, see Ratchford, *Web of Childhood*, pp. 99–132. Significant continuous portions are in Charlotte's "Zamorna's Exile" and "Caroline Vernon," available in

mutual enmity and fascination; between them, Percy and Douro mark the poles of Charlotte's adolescent conception of masculine grandeur.

The opening vignette has very little to do with the story that follows, but it does illustrate how seamless was Charlotte's conception of the affairs of this imaginary realm. For Edward and Julia Sydney flow into these opening pages from her earlier tale "The Foundling," although they are here reduced from romantic lovers to figures of domestic comedy.[10] This tonal shift is itself a pattern internal to the tale Charlotte's narrator tells in "The Secret," for the detached, ironic voice of Lord Charles is only intermittently dominant, emerging again from the rhapsodic flow of the narrative only to observe Douro at breakfast, Alexander Percy and Zenobia in their domestic discourse, or, more faintly, to record the mildly farcical conclusion of the melodrama. This oscillation is frequent in the juvenile tales and would seem to reflect an attempt to gain a controlled perspective on powerfully emotional materials. The framing of romantic love against a background of blackmail, bigamy, and deceit prefigures *Jane Eyre* in several ways, as do the evocation of atmosphere and setting, the suggestion of fairy tale, and the intrusion of the supernatural. Only with the creation of Jane herself, however, would Charlotte find a narrator capable at once of responding wholly to the potential of such material and subordinating it to the discipline of a mature and occasionally sardonic intelligence.

Here, however, in the early stages of the Angrian cycle, Charlotte's developing inventive faculty strains to lay the most excruciating tortures upon her most pathetic heroine: what worse for poor Marian, whose only strength is her love for Douro, than to discover in the early years of her marriage that she is still bound by a childhood betrothal to a man long thought dead? and that her natural father is not Alexander Hume but Alexander Percy, a vicious degenerate and her husband's bitterest enemy? It is an elaborate hoax, we find, but Charlotte uses it to dabble with themes of incest and bigamy. Out of such melodramatic materials comes the most extended portrait of Charlotte's first heroine, who is soon to disappear, however, as Charlotte seeks less innocent, more complexly motivated women to set against Douro's erotic energy. Mary Percy, Alexander's daughter, will succeed her in Douro's affections: Marian can only languish

---

Ratchford, *Legends of Angria.* "Caroline Vernon" has been re-edited and published in a more complete form by Winifred Gérin, *Five Novelettes* (London, 1971).

10. Wise and Symington, 8:220.

and die, but in Mary's future lie Douro's liaisons with Mina Laury and Caroline Vernon, which will evoke in her resolute stratagems to claim her due.[11] Mina Laury, we might observe in passing, stands in this story in much the same inferior relation to Douro as will Jane Eyre to Rochester. In later narratives, Mina develops into Douro's devoted mistress: resilient, capable, utterly selfless, she is at his side in another period of civil strife and during his subsequent exile.

The brothers Percy who appear here are among the several sons of Alexander who figure in the Angrian cycle. All apparently suffer from their father's unnatural hatred and persecution. In various combinations they afford Charlotte opportunity to develop themes through contrasting pairs; the brothers Crimsworth of *The Professor* are recognizable descendants of this early family, the mercenary Edward of this story evolving into a grasping merchant in Verdopolis and finally into Edward Crimsworth.[12] Henry Percy, however, until the discovery of this tale, had been known only through Charlotte's "Stanzas on the Fate of Henry Percy" (1834). As Fannie Ratchford noted, this poem posed a curious problem in the Angrian cycle, for it came after the death of Marian Hume but recorded her childhood betrothal to Henry Percy—her posthumous husband, Ratchford termed him.[13] Now, however, we can see that Charlotte's conception was not so laxly organized; for the early marriage had emerged in "The Secret" prior to the poem, as Charlotte sought narrative situations to test her radically simple heroine. The "Stanzas" then mark a return to "The Secret"; Charlotte re-creates in the poem Marian's painful transition from childish to adult love as perceived by Percy in his dreams aboard ship in the South Seas. Poem complements tale point for point, as the later work verifies the death (at his father's command) that Henry's ghost had attested in "The Secret."

---

11. "Passing Events" and "Caroline Vernon," ed. Gérin, *Five Novelettes*.

12. This sequence is traced nicely by Ratchford, *Web of Childhood*, pp. 190–200. Edward Percy later marries Maria Sneaky, who appears in the opening pages of this story—and who is sister to John of Fidena of "Lily Hart."

13. Ratchford, *Web of Childhood*, p. 88. At about the same time, Charlotte creates a parallel adolescent marriage for Douro—to Helen Victorina, who dies in childbirth (Ratchford, *Web of Childhood*, p. 85).

"Lily Hart"   As in the previous tale, the narrator is Lord Charles,
                although his presence is nowhere so marked as in the
                satiric passages of "The Secret." The circumstances
arising in "Lily Hart" presumably occur some years before the events of
"The Secret." If we assume a more-or-less coherent conception of the
history of the Glasstown Confederacy developed by Charlotte and
Branwell, we can place "Lily Hart" in the context of the great civil war de-
scribed by Branwell in "Letters from an Englishman."[14] The insurrection is
described as beginning on 16 March 1831, the narrator at the moment be-
ing in the company of the Marquis of Douro and Prince John of Fidena,
who rush immediately into the fray. It is in this first day of fighting, pre-
sumably, that Charlotte begins her domestic drama with the discovery of
the wounded Mr. Seymour, later revealed as Fidena. The rebellion was
fomented by Alexander Rogue, Branwell's creation who became the
Alexander Percy of "The Secret" and other narratives.

If we allow for minor discrepancies, Charlotte's tale meshes tidily with
Branwell's earlier war story. The false identities assumed by Fidena and
Douro are required for secrecy, for Verdopolis was for a brief spell occupied
by the rebels, who would no doubt have imprisoned or executed these two
captains of the government forces. During the two months of Seymour's
convalescence, the capital would have been retaken by the government,
and the year's interval during which Lily sinks into poverty would have
seen the great provincial Battle of Fidena, in which Rogue was finally
defeated by government forces under John of Fidena. From this victory, we
must then assume, he comes to claim his bride. Douro himself takes his
bride in this interval, as we know from Charlotte's "The Bridal,"[15] in which
the narrator places their nuptials shortly after the beginning of the Great
Rebellion. However, in "The Spell,"[16] a story that casts a problematical light
over all of her tales of Douro, Charlotte creates a twin brother for her hero,

14. T. J. Wise and J. A. Symington, eds., *The Miscellaneous Unpublished Writings of
Charlotte and Patrick Branwell Brontë*, 8:96. The Brontë children were doubtless
much interested at this time in the debates preliminary to the Reform Bill of
1832.

15. Wise and Symington, 8:202.

16. Wise and Symington, 8:377; printed in facsimile; separate edition by G. E.
McLean, *The Spell: An Extravaganza. An Unpublished Novel by Charlotte Brontë*
(London, 1931). Citations are from this edition.

who at times acts in his stead: "My Lady of Fidena," he claims, "I was the acquaintance of Lily Hart and not Zamorna [i.e., Douro]."[17]

If Douro's identity is in this tale obscure, that of John of Fidena becomes more clear. He is erroneously identified as John Percy (thus Alexander Percy's son) in the first published version of "The Spell"; this mistake is repeated in the Shakespeare Head edition of Brontë juvenilia,[18] perhaps because in "A Peep into a Picture Book" his portrait follows those of Alexander Percy and Zenobia, and he is referred to as "the son of Alexander."[19] As the closing scene of "Lily Hart" makes clear, however, his father Alexander is really Alexander Sneaky, King of Sneachieland and one of The Twelve—the original set of named soldiers who founded the Glasstown Confederacy. The Maria Sneaky of "The Secret" is his sister, as is the Lady Edith of "Lily Hart," also referred to in "The Spell."[20] The child John Augustus Sneaky appears also in "A Peep into a Picture Book" and with Douro's son Ernest in "A Brace of Characters."[21]

More important, however, than fixing John of Fidena among his proper relations is recognizing him as an early study for another John, the religious idealist St. John Rivers of *Jane Eyre*. This tall, grave young man with the lofty forehead, piercing eyes, and powerful mind is marked by the same reserve, the same sense of exalted standards. The hints of character we find in this tale of Fidena's betrothal are made explicit in "A Peep into a Picture Book," where he is referred to as "the Royal Philosopher."

How grave! what severe virtue! what deep, far-sought and well-treasured wisdom! what inflexible uprightness! Integrity that Death could not turn from the path of right; Firmness that would stoop to the block rather than yield one jot of its just, mature, righteous resolution; Truth from which the agonies of the wheel would be powerless to wring a word of equivocation; and to speak verity, Pride that could be no more thawed than the icebergs of Greenland. . . . the virtues pictured in his stately features seem of that high and holy order which almost exempt

---

17. *The Spell*, p. 142.

18. *The Spell*, p. xliv; Wise and Symington, 9:491.

19. Wise and Symington, 8:359.

20. *The Spell*, p. 143.

21. Wise and Symington, 8:361, 9:50. Ernest's mother was Helen Victorina (see note 13, "The Secret"). Ernest, not to be confused with Marian's child, Julius, was later murdered in Mina Laury's arms by Douro's enemies.

their possessor from sympathy with mankind. Thoughts of martyrs and patriots, and zealous but stern prophets . . . recur to our minds.[22]

And when we observe that in "Lily Hart" the situations of Jane and Rivers are simply reversed—he the mysterious stranger in distress, she the ministering samaritan—we get some sense of the long preparation out of which *Jane Eyre* grew.

Finally, the two tales in this manuscript come together when we learn—again from "A Peep into a Picture Book"—that John of Fidena was Marian Hume's most trusted and most loyal friend. Often, we are told, she sat at his feet in conversation with him and his wife Lily; and in the dark days when she languished from Douro's neglect, he tended her faithfully until her death.

> On quitting the bedside, as he hung over his adopted sister for the last time, a single large tear, the only one anguish, bodily or mental, ever wrung from the exalted soul of the Christian philosopher, dropped on the little worn hand he held in his; and he muttered half aloud: "Would to God I had possessed this treasure; it should not thus have been thrown away."[23]

This intersection, however, merely closes one orbit in the complex cycle of tales that occupied Charlotte Brontë in her formative years. The reconstruction by now is substantial; but there are fragments yet to be retrieved, which, like these, once comprised the virtual universe that was the daily realm of her imaginative life.

---

22. Wise and Symington, 8:358–59.
23. Wise and Symington, 8:360.